Insides Out

A BREAKING FREE...

SARA JO BOWLING

ArLu Publishing

Insides Out / A Breaking Free...
Published by ArLu Publishing
Salem, AR

Copyright ©2019 by Sara Jo Bowling. All rights reserved.

No part of this book may be reproduced in any form or by any mechanical means, including information storage and retrieval systems without permission in writing from the publisher/author, except by a reviewer who may quote passages in a review.

All images, logos, quotes, and trademarks included in this book are subject to use according to trademark and copyright laws of the United States of America.

ISBN: 978-0-578-90723-9
AUTOBIOGRAPHY / Personal Memoirs

Cover Photo @ 2019 www.gettyimages.com. All rights reserved – used with permission.

QUANTITY PURCHASES: Schools, companies, professional groups, clubs, and other organizations may qualify for special terms when ordering quantities of this title. For information, email sarabowling55@gmail.com.

All rights reserved by Sara Jo Bowling and ArLu Publishing.

Printed in the United States of America.

Introduction

Dear Readers,

The writings in this book took place from September 2017 through January 2019. It was during this period of my life that much unexpected growth occurred, for the positive. The first writing was written a couple of months after my mother had died. The content expresses some of my feelings and emotions with regard to her death. Then later, the experience of my father's decline and death was an impetus for written word. My parents shared good health and happiness for many years. I was blessed to have had such a loving, caring and dedicated mother and father. Thank you God for giving me an uncommonly wonderful couple, that I could call parents.

Another source of my expression during this year and a half span, was experiencing more freedom from psychiatric disorders. I had already reached a certain stability. But besides just being stable, I started to truly overcome all the excess psychological trappings that come with the disorders. It was during this time, I began to understand and experience confidence. I also had a great revelation that my person had always maneuvered from a point of negativity. That knowledge has led to continued change and an allowance of security and maturity. I am extremely thankful for the medical professionals in my life, past and present. My, what an understatement! Mental Health Care saved my life, and gave me a life! Thank you God for giving these people the understanding and skill, to help me learn how to be happy, content and at peace. I ask you to bless them and their lives. Much gratitude.

Since my life has really started to settle, I have begun to write of other topics besides emotions and the mental. WOW!!! Some of my writings refer to my hometown and experiences growing up. God has allowed me to capture and hold tight fond memories of my past. Despite the fact that much internal darkness existed at the time. Power Over Disorders!!!! YES!!!! Unbelievable. So Thankful.

The compilation of these writings are in chronological order. I write as I live. It is not a story as such. But it is the chapters of my everyday life. I usually write in reaction. I may be trying to solve a problem, vent, thank, reminisce or extinguish pain and fear. Uncertainty of the future, living with loss, possibilities of romance, concern for our country, are a few of the basis for topic. Some may be quite obvious and others extremely vague. *Insides Out*, is a continuation of self-expression found in my first book, *Feel The Mind, Touch The Heart*. Fortunate for me, there is much positive emotional growth. Also, the development of my writing skill and style is evident. But both books stand alone. It is not necessary to read the first in order to grasp the second. Present is the evolving of an enjoyable life…for me! From the depths of despair, now years later I'm living what I could have never dreamed. It just keeps getting better. Giving God the Praise!

To my family and friends… A Big Thank You! I love you all. You are so special and important. Yes, I continue to be blessed. Special thanks to my cousin Jessica, and her computer skills in compiling this book. Impossible without you! Aunt Gaye, I'm thankful for your time and *extra set of eyes*. And once more…Thank You God!

This book is dedicated to Betty in Viola, and Betty in Batesville. Love you both.

In memory of Momma and Daddy. Also, my dear friend Forrest. Heaven's Gain!

With hope and peace,
Sara

Note: I take advantage of poetic license when using ellipsis. They are my way of letting the flow of my thoughts, pause and pick up in written form.

Contents

Introduction	i
Death...hmmm	1
Awkward Love	4
Why Must We Change The Way We Feel?	6
When You Can Breathe	9
Therapist	11
First Holiday In Heaven	16
Welcome To The World	19
When Things Are Good	21
My Career	24
Dark Holiday	31
I'm Tired...Simply	33
Not To Figure	34
Fear Falling	36
Hey! I Kinda Like Me.	39
Ridin' High	42
What Is Happening?	44
Cake	46
Quiet Quite	47
Cries Heard	48
Daddy without Momma	50
Out Of Me	52
Solitaire	55
Discomfortable	57
Talkin' bout the Olympics	58
No Poles	62
From Here	63
What Can One Be?	65

Looking Outward	66
Escaping Fear	68
Why Does There Have To Be Somethin'?	71
Swirling Words	73
Why Not?	75
My Definition	77
See The Stain	79
A Circus	82
Better?	84
Out Of A Problem	87
Neutral	89
Why Moves	90
Blind Mind	92
Minus Torment	94
Forever Highway	96
High School Radio	98
Layer Of Dread	100
What Can Be?	102
A Second Mind	103
Cousin	104
You Know I Know...and I probably do.	106
Come So Far	109
LoveLife	111
Let Freedom Ring	113
My Jesus	115
Nobody In The Neighborhood	118
Solid	120
Rice and Refineries	122
Stalled	125
From Beaumont To Salem	127
Humbly, We Walk	133

The Most Important Man	135
Shades of Mourning	137
Homemade Ice Cream	139
Too Much Me	140
Empty Canvas	142
Once Burning	144
Our Own Beach	146
Little Bird	148
Dirty Hair	149
Floatin' In Space	152
My Sister And I	155
I Want To Care	157
Lightning Strikes	159
Blood Red Moon	160
Evaporating	161
Bowling Hill Nights	163
More, More!!!	168
Own It!	170
Brief Thoughts for the "Feel-Good"	171
Seein' After	172
Limbo	176
The Element of Fear	179
Shoestrings	182
Stepped Out For A Spell	184
Wandering...Wondering	186
When There's Nothing To Hold Onto	188
Doe...A Deer	190
Where Am I Goin'?	191
Just Feel It	193
Time Forward	195
Passion's Friend	197

Get Gone!	198
My Street...Wooten Road	199
The Flame of Shame	203
When You Get To Say "Thank You"	205
This Quiet Winter	207
Cultivating Identity	209
I Never Knew...And Now I Do	211
The Evolving Door	214

Death...hmmm

So dreaded. So feared. So paralyzing.
So bizarre. So creepy. So eerie.
What we don't know. What we'll never
know...until...It's Us! I guess the only
way to even get a glimpse, is watching
another *take the next step*. Death.

Throughout life there have been words
of heaven and hell. To scare. To prevent.
To calm. To reassure. To ostracize. To
lay guilt. To claim promise. Oh...the
manner of how spoken and when addressed,
could determine the impact and sway.

For this one, death always held a fast grip.
There was plenty of exposure to funerals...
memorials, observance of the body lifeless.
There were appropriate periods of mourning,
however conflicting the statement. Yet, it
was always there...waiting to happen.
Happen to me. Happen to them.

Finally. It happened...to her. The person who
gave me the most security in this life of 55 years.
Not that I had to have constant contact, presence,
affirmation or lead. But she...she always had been.
Always. Surely the loss would have downward
impact. Fearful times would await. But no?

Her life of disassociated sleeping lasted two weeks. Her body continued to breathe and breathe. Even when we wanted to let her go...she remained. Her sister saw it. We were trying to *time* God. How human we were. Wanting to rid our discomfort as if we were in command.

The three of us surrounded her late night. Her sister, my sister and myself. The wiser, always the eldest, suggested prayer. A prayer to readjust to God's timetable. We each took turns and spoke aloud "in your time and your will." We opened our eyes after spoken words. Right then...with three short, peaceful and relaxed breaths her spirit lifted to heaven.

All my life of fifty-five, I saw and watched my mother live. And with 5 to 6 years of decline, culminating to 2 weeks of dying...I saw and watched my mother die. What happened with her last breath? I raised my hands and arms in the air rejoicing and said "Hallelujah!"

So the fear, the dread, the eeriness. Witnessing the last years of my mother's life, gave me so much strength to be a part of her death. And truly, *she beat death*. Our Lord paved the way. Her belief. Her faith. Her witness. A preparation for entry into the heavenly afterlife.

And for me...am I still scared of death? Well, yes... to a degree. But it no longer holds the power it once did. The thing I most likely feared in life has already happened...losing her. And it's ok. I'm ok. My mother. My mother taught me how to live. And my mother taught me how to die. And my aunt reminded us...it's all in God's Time.

Awkward Love

Why the nausea? Why the semi-fear? There is no harm pending. In retrospect, no attack on person has ever occurred. The embarrassment can't help but tinge what would otherwise be a normal reaction. Oh...that's it. Something has been done which drives one to hide in a type of shame. Is it possibly borderline wrong? Well, the searching reveals no *bad*. So why? Why the natural instinct to retreat to an alone safe place? As if safety is needed. That's it...you're alone...so it's gotta be safe. Hmmm. Or maybe instead of retreating, there is a shuffling of apprehensive emotion. The use of sarcasm as a deflector can always assure escape.

So, what is one running from? There has been delving and sorting...trying and sizing...remembering and dismissing...culling over and over. What is it that causes one to break away full speed ahead? Love. Huh??? More specifically...the reception of love.

Love...the greatest of all. Why on earth is there fear of love? Well, it's the things that can come with it. Closeness, affection, a soothing aspect, loyalty, attention, encouragement, praise, compliments... these all can tag along with love. UGH!!!! Why? Why despise what is meant to feel good?!! There is always the notion that we somehow believe *good feelings* are a luxury. Only to be possessed by the truly deserving. But who is to say who deserves what? Surely, we are not to blame God for letting us feel good! Oh my...what a messy mixture of half-truths and false perceptions of God and ourselves. That's it...it can be such a big mess, when we try to analyze and make sense of emotions that test our internal observation of our being.

Well, the answer is not clear...why the fear of love and its symptoms. Sounds like a disease! Damn! Even so, at this point there is much, much more delightful acceptance of love than prior stages of life. Perhaps, it's not the *deserving* aspect of the issue...but rather being *comfortable* with love and its properties. That's it. There is no conflict of belief systems or past actions. It's just letting oneself be at ease with endearment. Therefore, forget the quest to *find out why* or understand the unsettling reactions to love. Just let it be. Don't fight it. There may be periods of awkwardness inside, and step backward in the process. But I'm betting the more love in its complete form becomes familiar, the easier to digest. WOW!!! Did I just say that?? Sounds like I'm comparing self-acceptance to the dietary! Hahaha. Well, anyway...things are *lighter* now. Love is not a fear to conquer. Rather, it is an allowance of **feel-good**. Wonderful! I don't have to figure it out...I just have to get used to it!

Why Must We Change The Way We Feel?

At times, why do we want to change the way we feel? So we'll feel better, of course. I've been told there are four root feelings: mad, sad, glad and scared. Now, that's just Layman's Psychology 101...not going into a lot of depth. At any rate, that covers the basics. Just about always when we are feeling good and happy, there is no desire to change. When we are scared, we definitely want to feel safe. Makes sense. Then when we're mad... and we finally get it out of our system, we're ok. And no one wants to be sad in the depressed, hurting sense. Sometimes we feel a bit of melancholy, usually related to memories...and basically we let ourselves feel and then it passes.

Let's go further and consider a sense...that in a way can *revolve* around the basic feelings. The one that stands out most glaring is *uneasy* or *uneasiness*. Lack of ease. We don't feel real bad, but we don't feel good in a solid sense. Of course, there can be uneasy feelings towards differences of opinions and possible danger. But what if we are just going through the day...and we feel...uncomfortable with our being? The first instinct is to question...What is wrong? But does there have to be something wrong? Not really. Sometimes we are just gonna feel unsteady, unreal, unfamiliar, a bit anxious. Now...maybe a lot of you do not deal with this type of...well...crap! But for some of us who tend to *feel* everything...heightened senses, it can disrupt the normal routine of the day. For me, I'm learning when uneasiness comes...*just go with it*. Don't fight it. Don't try to drown it. Don't try to beat it down. Let it happen. Let it run its course. Sure, it's uncomfortable. But eventually, the unwelcomed feeling will dissipate. Who in thu hell ever said we're gonna feel good and ok all of the time? And that if we don't feel good and ok...something is wrong with us? NOBODY!!!!!! Oh...I guess most of us were raised that we should feel steady and stable, all a part of being a responsible adult who is doing the *right thing*...whatever that may be. But NO. We can be doing great. *All our ducks are in a row.* And then for some reason or another...we feel a bit uneasy. That's it! I just wrote "for some reason or another"... We have to come to accept that we are not always gonna know the reasons for our feelings. And that's ok. It's got to be ok or else we'll drive ourselves nuts trying to figure out what can't be resolved.

So, to summarize. I wrote this writing because right now I feel *uneasy*. Nothing's wrong. I'm in good health. Things are going good. There are no stresses. Situations of life come and go...and I deal with them up front. It's just for some of us *who can feel a leaf drop*...we have to realize that's just a part of our personal make-up. It's in our genes...or whatever...who knows??? In the end, it doesn't matter. The *dis ease* will pass. It will eventually be gone. And it may not come back for a good while. But rest assured, it will come back. Then again...we just *let it do its thing*. Try to occupy our minds, before our minds are occupied with an obsession of the uneasiness. Work with our hands, change the subject, or help another person. If we are not able to *derail it*... just let it be. Usually it won't last too long...then it will just leave. Just as I am finishing this writing...it has almost passed! Thanks for listening!

When You Can Breathe

Clear silence. Soft light.
Such an ease of living never imagined.
Fragmented thought is not the devil.
No longer a fierce competition for sanity.

Smoothness continues to settle daily.
Not so much calamity, rather calmness.
Reactions...minus the *knee-jerk*.
Can it really be this good?

Wait. *Stuff* still happens. But the
response is usually level. Of course,
the occasional *freak-out*. And the
snappy, irritable and angry attitude...
yeah...maybe more often than realized.

Oh my...how things have changed.
The coarse introspect diminished to
simple question of reason. No longer
the framed self-destruction.

Caution...yes. Must keep watch to
protect the acquired and prevent a
backslide. Such is life for everyone.
But the guard is of a kind nature.

The mind now whispers. And the
content usually positive and desirable.
God has had mercy. Thanks to give.
Praise for the second, minute and hour
that one once despised.
When You Can Breathe.

Therapist

It's a last resort...and they're there.
Listening, caring, stabilizing, comforting.
You're at the bottom...they are only a type
of balm. Not even a glimmer of hope.
God help...anything for the pain.

The haze lifts a bit. You see they have a
face. They are a human being. But honestly,
aren't they...but a *trapped ear*? Funny...
they continue to be at the same place
and the same time. They don't run away.

You smile. They smile. What's this?
You feel a bit of ease. Oh, how you've
longed for some type of relief. But they
have no idea who you are. They are just
a stranger with a diploma on their wall.

You anxiously wait for the appointed
date. You talk with more freedom. You
kinda laugh. They are fun to be around.
They are consistent. The same person
every week. Jekyll and Hyde...they aren't.

Possible to trust? You take a chance.
All is well. Everything is safe. You are
safe. They are a *friend* of sorts. Do
they have any idea how important they
are to you? You're sure not gonna let
them know.

One day they mention words that hurt
your ears. They are talking more and
more about feelings and emotions. YUCK!!!!
Why did they have to spoil everything?!!
You're frustrated. NO...damn it! You're mad!!
You're not gonna talk anymore. A minute passes...
and you speak.

You continue to look forward to your
meetings with them. But it's confusing. It's so
easy to get angry with them. But something
keeps you coming back. Well...you have been
feeling a bit better and safer. But shit! What's
so important about things in your past?

You say words you thought would never
escape your being. And they remain. They
are not running or reprimanding. They listen.
This person is really unusual. You tend to
think highly of them...even if they irritate you.
They begin to be special.

What's this? You haven't had a blind eye...
but you hadn't given it much thought...
They talk to other people! You see people
come and go from their office. Are they as
significant as you? Are you as significant as
them? What a sorry-assed two-timer! Why did
you let them in?!

Even so, you continue to make an appearance.
They have your attention...you have their attention.
That's what you like best...their attention. You've
yelled, shouted, cussed, laughed, argued and thanked.
But hell if you'll ever cry! They can't make you cry!
Of course, they never mention it. But you just
know...somewhere in those feelings there is crying.
When Hell Freezes Over!!!!!!!!!!!!!

You're in deep. You've shown your cards.
You begin to acknowledge fear that brings on the
pain. You're talking too much. You stomp your
feet. Kinda throw a fit. They don't condone, but
they don't make you leave. In fact, they say you
deserve to feel the way you feel. UGH!!!! Feelings!!

You realize there is a line. You can only be so close.
How Unfair!!! You're giving them everything inside...
but you only get crumbs about their person. You've
come to understand it is the way this particular
relationship works. But Damn...Unfair!!!! Kinda hurts.
Mad! You continue to appear...same time next week.

Time passes. Life happens. Things are not as hard. But there's something. You continue to make the appointment. You haven't done it intentionally, but you've slowly put them on a pedestal. Even so, you know they can only be human. Struggles occur, problems arise and they are there to listen and advise. You like them. They are a good being.

You go a bit deeper. A place you've never been before. This is shaky. Shame flickers even if it is not deserved. Awkwardness. For you, it has not been a matter of yours or another's morality. Even so, you feel much guilt. Hmmm. This is what you've felt all your life. The mind, the soul shreds. And you cry. They remain. You remain.

You have grown close to this paid confidant. Not long ago...how you would strive for their approval. You would take any hint of compliment. You wanted to be their world...even though you knew that made no sense. So, you just went through the motions, did the work, felt the feelings. You began to realize what you could be.

So, you walk into their office. You're confident. A happiness and peace are becoming more familiar to your everyday life. Trials arise and you overcome...using tools they have taught you. You no longer expect too much from them. They compliment...and you simply say "thank you." Ha! How about that? You no longer have to have their approval. But oh how good it feels!

You have grown. Not only have you healed from the onset...but you continue to develop in the positive. You're not sure...but it seems they've let just enough of their guard down... for you to see more of their person. But the line remains. You're glad it does...so goes the relationship. They listen. They care. They advise. They encourage. They hold their position and you are equal.

First Holiday In Heaven

It's Momma's first Thanksgiving away. She's in heaven, ya know. Left earth several months ago. I figure she's doin' fine. But I wonder if she's in charge of the dressing? I mean, she usually was for our neighborhood and family celebrations.

Wonder who she'll sit with at the table? Grandpa, Grandma, Harlin, Hala, Marx for sure. Gaye's still with us. In fact, I'll be eating the turkey meal with her. Oh...there are so many from our family who are up there. Plus friends...and probably earthly enemies who are now friends. Funny how that works!

I do hope Mrs. Crow will bake her sweet potato pie. And Zeila will definitely be able to come up with something delicious. It would be interesting to know how many calories are in heaven's foods. Cause neither one of those neighbors cooked skimpy.

Who'll say the blessing??? I mean...
will it be a fight? God, Jesus and all
the disciples...plus those ministers that
thought themselves so eloquent. I know.
I'm bein' kinda tacky. But anyhoo…

Well, I'm sure there'll be a lot of talkin'
around the table. I wonder if it will be one
big table. Lordy! They may have those
brown metal folding chairs like we had
at church. If you were a little girl, the
metal was cold to your legs. If you were
a teenage girl, they would snag your
pantyhose. Ugh!

I'm sure the feast will be just that.
Plenty of leftovers too. Kinda like the
fish and loaves. At any rate, somebody
is gonna have to wash the dishes. Or
do they have automatic dishwashers in
heaven? Hmmm.

So, everybody is satisfied and full.
For sports fans it's time for some
football! YAY!!! Who's playin'?
The Cardinals and Saints...of course.
I know Momma doesn't care. She's
not into athletics in any shape, form or
fashion. Eventually, she'll stretch out
on the couch and work a crossword.

Well, Momma...it's your first holiday in heaven. I hope you enjoy yourself. Everything down here is just fine... considering it is earth. I'm not in any hurry to see you...but it's good to know that one day I'll get to taste your pecan pie again! Truly...someday it will be a Thanksgiving Forever and For Everybody!

Welcome To The World

You always knew you were equal.
Sure that you were *as good as*.
It was imbedded in your upbringing.
Always *just as important as*.

But your life...not so sure. Not
very steady. No finished products.
Just floating in the paths of everyday
humanity. Nothing to stake a claim.

And the internal chaos...so extreme.
Heights and depths...how great the range.
Your reality was not of average substance.
Strange, peculiar moods and behaviors.
So it was.

Then there was stability. A steadiness
never before known. It took you awhile...
getting used to the *new norm*. Slowly
you began to believe in yourself...not just
a human being...but a deserving soul.

You've done something! A contribution.
You're beginning to *fit in*. This world...
there is a space for you. You've made a
mark. It even has your name on it!

Well...Welcome to the world. You've got a place. Oh...you know you've always belonged...But you didn't *feel* a part.
It will be interesting to see how your life develops from this point.

I'll say it again...Welcome to the world. You're feeling what a good life should feel. What'd you say? Never in your wildest dreams? Much Gratitude.

When Things Are Good

What do you write when things are good? Huh? Well, most of my writing has been a result of trying to win at the battle of life. And most of it has been chaotic, crisis-type shit. So...hmmm.

Tonight I want to write. Things are good. It's officially Christmas Eve 2017. So much better than any other holiday season of my life. Really? FOR SURE!!!!!! Wait...I don't want to get negative while I'm trying to write something positive!

I could say it's a sad time because it's the first Christmas without my mother. But that wouldn't be true. Well, last night it kinda bothered me...but not really and not for any length of time. I'm glad Momma's in heaven. She had a good long life. Even through her years of dementia she seemed to enjoy most of her days. Merry Christmas Momma!

Should I be down because I'm not surrounded by kids and grandkids for the holidays? Hell no! I never wanted children...except for some fleeting moments of which I felt my biological clock ticking away. I mean, I love my nieces and nephews. And great nieces and great nephews. But I can only take them in spells. They don't live near me, so when I do see them it's really enjoyable.

What about a significant other? What's up with that? Good Lord...I've just now got my life on track. I don't need somebody to screw it up! I'm so used to being alone and being single. And I like it. Of course, if it were meant to be...it would be! Right? But it's not like I'm *pining away*. Just hoping for someone to kiss under the mistletoe, so my holiday would be complete. No...I've got it good like it is!

Well, Daddy is stuck in the nursing home. Wait... I don't look at it that way. He's where he can get the best care possible, according to what I could do for him. Sure, there are downsides to such facilities. But you *call their number* when you need to. And I usually see him every day. Not that it's a burden. I just happen to live close and it's enjoyable...most of the time. I plan on going to eat Christmas Dinner with him. I'm sure it will be delicious. BAHAHAHA!!!!! Oh well.

Santa Claus? Who? Presents? What?
Well...I've never been very materialistic and that's a damn good thing! Honestly, I've been counting my blessings for a good while now. Seriously! Oh...my aunt and I will exchange gifts that we picked out ourselves. SURPRISE!!! Yeah...well. Anyway, that's covered...I'm good with that. And of course, I have a couple gifts for my Dad. So... HO! HO! HO!

Life Goals. WOW!!!! I've achieved a life goal just recently. Up until this one, there had been only one other benchmark accomplishment. That's not saying I haven't been a successful person. But it is what it is. And I've truly been enjoying the pleasure this achievement has brought. AND... I look for it to continue to be a *feel-good* for a while. YAY!!

My health. There's always the wish for good health. And as far as I'm concerned, I'm healthier than I've ever been in my entire life. Of course, it has nothing to do with scales, exercise and fitness. Lord help me! No. I don't have my *college years' bod!* But my mind... well...what can I say? THANK THE LORD for sanity!!!! Totally serious! And I know you know how serious I am.

Well. Hmmm... I did have something to write even though I'm not in dire straits. And it was all good. And it *is* all good. So what should I do? Say *Thanks!* Gratitude to friends and family. Grateful for my way of life and all that goes with it. So thankful for being blessed in numerous ways. And Thank You God... for the meaning of Christmas! Away In A Manger. SILENT NIGHT. Peace...ahh...

My Career

What do you want to be when you grow up? What?? I had no idea. I couldn't even conceive of being an adult. I was just struggling to stay halfway sane. A lot of time inside my head, I would *live out* people that I had just imagined. Actually, that was a very important coping mechanism for me as I tried to avoid collisions in my mind. I mowed a lot of yards in my early years. In high school I continued to mow lawns and tacked on a productive stint at a fast food chicken restaurant. Oh yeah...can't forget those episodes of babysitting! HAHAHA... SO not a mother!

So, on to college. What was the plan? Well, what else? Do what my older sister did! Leave Beaumont, choose home economics as a major and meet the guy you will marry. ALL in one freshman year! It worked for her. Hmmm. Well, I got the part about leaving Beaumont down. I mean I took it to the hilt...all the way to Fayetteville, Arkansas. WOOO PIG! I survived my first year of college. I survived! I actually made pretty good grades. I took the required beginning courses and one home economics textile course. Lordy! Besides making a pattern for a piece of clothing, we had to look under a microscope and determine the type of fiber...just by the ends of the strand. HARD!!! Well, the second semester of my freshman year, I was more realistic...I started studies in Health Education. But we won't go into mental health...just yet! Spring semester of 1981 had some good points...but by the end of March, I was severely depressed. Of course, I didn't know it. It just was. So, that was enough college.

Back in Beaumont I started working at Gateway Walgreen's as a cashier. God Help Me! I'm not a *numbers person*. I don't know if my drawer ever balanced on the first try! That lasted about a year, then all the demons crashed in on me. Yes...The Depression. For old timer's sake...My Nervous Breakdown! So began my trek into reality and sanity...not that I was to stay on course. No...Forever a gradual climb to *Self-Actualization!* Thank you Maslow. haha I did make an "A" in psychology. But that was after I returned to college...after Walgreen's...after "The Breakdown."

So, I'm now in school at Lamar University in Beaumont...living at home with my parents. Ok. I continue the Health Education route and add Physical Education as my major. Now...I am getting more into reality! I was able to get a good part-time job in a USDA lab at the Texas A&M Rice Experiment Station near China, Texas. My side of town. Perfect. Well, all this time I'm receiving psychiatric help. Medications and therapy. At one point, I dropped a semester and received inpatient care for about three months. A very productive hospitalization. It was then I started being interested in psychotherapy as a possible career. BAHAHA. But I knew I needed to *grow* more. Perhaps??? Also, from time to time I'd help my dad with his side business...crop consulting. Go out into rice and soybean fields. Swing parachute material nets back and forth and collect insects. The amount of a particular insect and its growth stage, led my dad to be able to tell the farmer if it was worth spraying the fields with insecticide. Yeah...saw some snakes. AND the trail of an alligator tail!! YIKES!

December 1986, I graduated from Lamar with a B.S. in Physical Education and Health Education. I had the qualifications to teach. But I didn't have the confidence. So, in a 'roundabout way, I avoided all my fears...well. I started thinking...I'll get a job related to my major that will eventually lead me to getting a Master's Degree in Counseling through the education department. Thus... come out a *fine-tuned* psychotherapist! Sounded good.

My first *real* job. A recreation trainer at Richmond State School in Richmond, Texas. The pay wasn't great...but it had insurance. And the holidays were good. My job description was very *glorified*. I witnessed some of the most heartbreaking sights of humanity. But I kept thinking...this will be a stepping stone into my next job working with people. Again...leading to a psychotherapist profession. Yeah...well after about 8 months it lead to psychotherapists. AND again I was the one *lying on the couch*. After a lengthy hospitalization, I was left without a job. And still very depressed. One could say that the job depressed me...and it did. But it wasn't the root cause of my clinical depression.

Back in Beaumont. Back in my parents' home. Ugh. It took a good year before I was able to get another *real* job. In the meantime, while I battled the depression...I did odd jobs on good days. Well, ends up...there was an opening as a lab technician in the USDA laboratory in which I had worked part-time in college. Me... scientific? Not really. Anyhoo...just mix the chemicals, etc. and do what I was told. A government job, good pay, insurance, good holidays. What more do I need? An apartment...Yay...I'm on my own again! Well... that lasted about 9 months...then major depression... again. Hospitalization... again. Loss of job...again. BUT I didn't end up in my parents' home again! No... they didn't want to live with me, and I didn't want to live with them. Not that we were mad at each other. Just the way we were. I am so fortunate. My dad found an old trailer...built the same year I was born! It was run down, but the trailer park was relatively safe. My parents bought the trailer for me and my dad made it livable. Actually, I don't think the door locks ever worked. But Hey...I'm alive today!!!

I lived in the old trailer for 8 years. Eight years which saw the onset of the manic side of my Bipolar Disorder. Oh My!! If that trailer could talk. Lordy! I had many odd, odd jobs during that time. Just to give you an idea... Worked as *runner* for a car parts store. I loved that job. But one day, when I hadn't slept for about 2 weeks, I was delivering a car part to a mechanic's garage...and I got lost. I knew Beaumont *like the back of my hand*...but not at that moment. Just so happened when I kinda regained composure, I looked up and I was right across the street from my psychiatrist's office! I walked into his office all sweaty, with probably the gaze of a madwoman. I walked past the receptionist, can't remember whether his door was opened...don't know if he had a patient in his office. I just remember slamming my fist on his desk and said... "Put me back on that stuff!!!" That "stuff" being lithium. We had been trying different avenues with my medication. He just looked up at me and kinda chuckled and said... "All right, all right." Hahaha. Needless to say, the job had ended. I don't really remember how I got back to the auto parts store. I just know I slept for about a month!

Also, during the trailer years I had a job as a handyman for an electrician/plumber/maintenance man. The highlight was changing air conditioning filters on top of Kentucky Fried Chickens and Burger Kings!! That really was fun...honest! Again...my temperament ended the less than desirable job. Oh...and then I was head of a crew...head of a crew of Domino's Pizza door hanger coupons, *door hanger-uppers*. Hahaha. I was the only one old enough to drive!!! BAHAHA. Well... that job lasted until I got bit by a dog. Meant a trip to the emergency room. Thank ya Momma and Daddy! Insurance? Really?? When I wasn't working odd jobs, I did some volunteer work at nursing homes and agencies...something to make me feel like I was being *a citizen*. And yes...I did honestly care for the cause at hand.

Well, my last *real* job occurred when I was living in the old trailer. I did all kinds of jobs for Thrifty Nickel Want Ads Paper. Delivering the paper, production, desk work, and finally outsides sales. I even had a *calling card!* And then again...in less than a year...dark depression. The job ended. That was in 1992. More odd jobs. Then I finally realized and accepted that I needed to be on disability for my Bipolar Disorder. I started receiving benefits in 1995. But I still tried to work odd jobs when I could. On two occasions when things were going better than usual...I still had my mind on becoming a psychotherapist. WHAT???!! Yes. I thought I was stable enough to get a job and get off of disability. Oh really? Well...evidently it wasn't ALL a pipe dream. I passed the GRE and enrolled in graduate studies at the University of Houston - Clear Lake. That lasted one semester. 4.0 GPA and still not sane! Bowed out graciously. Back to Beaumont...where later when I was on a *good swing* again...I tried graduate courses at Lamar University. After being totally humiliated when giving a paper in a statistics class...by the instructor questioning my analysis...I finally *let go* of becoming a psychotherapist. You're Welcome World!

September 2001 I moved to Salem, Arkansas. Since I've been here I've done a lot of odd jobs. Sitting with elderly people. Worked for a man who sold used furniture and such. At one point I was into buying and selling *junk* out of my little Dodge Dakota truck. The next Fred Sanford!! Lots of mood swings, etc., etc. Oh yeah...refurbishing old fishing rods/reels...learned my limits there! Detailing cars for a friend's used car lot. Oh...I could go on.

As I look at my *career* in life...there is a common thread that goes with the Bipolar Disorder. Paranoia. Yes...In retrospect, I can now look back and see where symptoms of paranoia have always played a part in the loss of jobs. I did not realize this aspect until the last couple years. I was helping a friend in kinda a part-time capacity with jobs in her store. The job didn't last but 2 months. As I dissected that job situation, I saw where I had *assumed* a lot that was not happening. Kinda scary. I never blatantly burned bridges during my work life. But there were times I would have rather not been seen again. Up until I realized how distorted my mind could be to me...I seemed to have a certain amount of guilt for not *really* working. But when I saw how I set myself up for failure, with an inability to change...attributed to an additional mental *hang up*...I've pretty much let go of the guilt.

Now...due to ALL the experiences and skills associated with my life careers and lack of career... Well...I Wrote A Book!!! Yes!!
And I have the perfect odd job...Giving rides, especially to senior citizens and the elderly...to doctor appointments, stores, errands, etc. Little room for paranoia in that time span! Life Is Good!!!!!

Dark Holiday

It is a holiday. A time for joy and hope.
But for some it will forever hold a darkness,
not deserved for any. A loss...so untimely.
A loss of breathing youth. The agony
and fear that must have taken hold of the
life departed...it confounds the survived.

Words witnessed by a stranger is a
reminder of so much lacked knowledge.
"No person could *drive me* to do that."
Maybe there is more to the tragedy than
one reason...as if that is not enough.
Perhaps the mind and soul had been severely
troubled over a long period of time. Or
maybe the reflex was instant, due to an all-
consuming fear. What does it matter?
Pain is Pain.

Other verbalization heard... "I don't see
how it could be that bad. If I was found,
they better start looking for the one who
did it." Does this person actually believe
they are immune to such *illness*? Maybe
they are...maybe their person doesn't feel
such heights and depths. True...we are all
different.

So what to make of it? The person is gone. The victims are those that remain. Compassion is a must. Because one does not understand in such a blind manner, does it mean they don't care? Not necessarily. Does it mean they are ignorant to the subject at hand? Definitely. We are responsible to not find ourselves so oblivious.

It's time. It's time that we allow our hearts and minds to sincerely look at this terminal disease. Who's next? A friend, family member or perhaps... God help us...not ourselves! No. There is no *vaccine* to be administered. The intervention must be wide-opened eyes and ears. Souls full of love and strength from above. And may we never ever pass judgment.

I'm Tired...Simply

I'm tired. But I'm not *worn out*.
I don't hurt or have a headache.
I've had plenty of sleep recently.
I'm just tired...I'm just good.

No. I haven't put in a hard day's work.
And I haven't *worked out* as in fitness.
I'm not *Fat and Lazy* tired.
I'm just tired...I'm just good.

How's this? I can now live and breathe...
carry out normal activities in a relaxed
mode. How foreign. How fresh!
I'm just tired...I'm just good.

You know...I'll bet it has something to
do with the inner workings of that
thing called the mind. How nice...
to not think and think...and think.
Am I exaggerating this new manner
of *being*? No!

I'm just tired...I'm just good.
I'm just positively good and tired!

Not To Figure

Not trying to figure it out...really.
Already have a good idea. Cause...
never ever to be totally understood.
So just go through the motions and
do *patchwork* to get by.

To get by. Not really honest
desperation. No. Far from it.
It's just the good...is not the best.
Wait. Not expecting *the best*
all the time.

So a problem exists. Yes. The familiar
adversary...a disorder trait. What
is it? Slight depression. Oh no. No...
Not bad. Not despair. Not demonic.
Not dark. Not eerie. Not pain.
Rather, a bit too lethargic.

The bed is too comfortable. That is
one way of making it simple. But
it can't be considered so trite. At first
thought...just really enjoying being
relaxed. And relaxed state is new
to the person. But getting out of hand.

Considerations: Tired? Lazy? Avoidance?
The length of time covers several months.
So...it's not *just going away*. Again.
It's simple. It's body chemistry. A slight
swing. A thread intertwined among much
stability. So tricky. An inconvenience?
That does not give enough respect to its
potential power.

What to do? See it for what it is.
Don't have to *figure it out*. Damn.
If one could only get a physical glimpse.
I mean...just a speck under a microscope
would be some justification. But not to
be. Forever invisible.

A call. An appointment. A visit.
A slight adjustment...probably all that
will be necessary. Praying that to be so.
So...it does not control. It does not
have to be figured out...Why? Because
it can't be *figured out*. Just know what
is. And know what has to be done.
No *beating up*. No extra distressing.

Next step. Only step. A call with hopes
of a cancellation. So much easier than
it used to be. Not excessive obsessive
thinking...trying to make rational. Forever
failure and sure demise. No. This depression...
again...simply...A thread intertwined among
much stability. Grateful for progress.

Fear Falling

Always lurking...even in the best
of times. The past. Good times.
Hard times. Accomplishments of
which to be proud. Love, pain,
positive excitement, *top of the
world* experiences. And fear...
always lurking.

Is it the same at this point in life?
Well...no. Oh, life happens.
Problems arise. But so does the good.
And many times...so does the great!
Wow! The notion...it hedges from
time to time. But it is now seen in
a different light. Even the *feel* is
different. Not so extreme. Not so
bizarre. Fear Falls.

The disorder. Once a rampant
expression of every negative emotion.
Suppression? No. Dissipation. Ahh...
nice. So thankful. Arrows continue to
be shot. Still a target for the insidious
disease. But a fortress has been built.
No. Not in one day. Fifty-six years
of combat. The war not over till the
afterlife. But now...winning battle
after battle. How wonderful. Grateful.
Fear Falls.

The person. At times so despised. Why?
Not felt to be *in sync* with belief system.
Such a torment. It will be death. Hiding
every thought, emotion, reaction. In all
actuality, hidden from no one. Let alone
the God worshiped. A recognition of
false perception over a lifetime, seems to
have brought entanglement with the spiritual.
No longer. Going out on a branch. Truly
trusting the Deity.
Fear Falls.

The next world. What will it hold? The past...
forever chaos brought on by the disorder. The
person and a heavy dose of religious persuasion
at a young age. Did I say spiritual persuasion?
No. Doctrine of man and emotional invasion
by humans. Yes...just humans. But wait.
At the same time there was the introduction
to true spirituality by those...*just loving humans*.
What will the next world hold? Don't know.
Will never know until that day. The unknown.
Such a fierce adversary to everyday life, when
not taken in stride. So, clinging to "Here is
my belief. Help my unbelief."
Fear Falls.

Living in the moment. Taking each breath with the flow of blood. Don't jump the gun. Don't try to *make be*. Just let happen. Help my brother. Make a difference for the good of all. Respect life. Live life. Love life. Accept love. Fear Falls.

Hey! I Kinda Like Me.

Hey! I kinda like me. Hmmm... Yes...I really seem to be in the positive. So strange. Is it wrong to think too highly of self? Well... Hold On! I just said *I kinda like me*. Oh...so your self-esteem is not out of hand. Ok. That's cool. That's acceptable.

But wait. Would it be bad if I really liked myself even more than *kinda*? God forbid I get the *big head*. No. Wait...there is nothing wrong with more than minutely liking me. For real? I think...I think so. Is that ok God? Huh? I'm asking my Creator if it's ok to really like what He made. Lordy Mercy! How crazy!

If you asked me if you should more than *kinda* like yourself...what would I say? (Did you follow that sentence?) Anyhoo...I'd tell you...Love yourself! God loves you and so do I. So why do I *hold out* on myself...my being? Arrogance. I'm not supposed to be arrogant. Who in thu hell is comparing having a love for self to be on the same plane as arrogance? Some, I guess. Me...Sometimes.

Do I have to prove anything to myself
to more than *kinda* like myself? No.
And honestly, for me that's never been
part of the equation. Actually, my dilemma
revolved around *my person*. Who I
was in regards to inner desires and identity.
Lord help us all. Don't even go there! It
is a dark evil place! Wow! What a
number on my human. Defeat from the
beginning. Hell awaits for sure. Oh...
Bullshit! There...I stated.

Well...it's a beginning...to *kinda* like
myself. More humane than the past.
You know...it must be ok to like one's
self. Really, it must be ok to love one's
self. This doesn't mean I think I'm better
than...or higher than my God. No. It
simply is being pleased with the person
who God made to hold my spirit. And
of course, there is plenty of room for
God's spirit in my person.

So, is God proud to be in my person?
Well...God are you? I kinda think I heard
Him say "yes." Again...at this point *kinda*.
Goodness sakes. Man...It sounds like I'm
dwelling on the bottom of a murky and muddy
lake. With scum settled on the surface.
Wait a minute. Give me a break. I'm just
getting used to letting God love all of me.

SO...Give me a break! Eventually, I'll learn to completely like and love myself. Always my love towards God first.

Years have passed and slowly I let God love me more and more. Ever since I asked Him into my life at age ten. Good grief. It's taken all these years for me to let God love all of me? Oh...I could look at it as such a sad state. But it's not! It's my life. It's how it has *played out*. My life has happened how it was supposed to have happened. Like it or not. So...there it is. At this point, I choose to like...and begin to love the way my life has processed. Man...That sounds kinda clinical! Oh well...it was the only word I could come up with...typing so fast. And it does make sense...and is the truth. So be it.

Well. So...I'm sure I *kinda* like me. And I'm steady goin' in the direction of loving all of self. ALL of my person. Just the way I was made. That is good. There is promise for a bright future. I already know happy. Now, I'm betting there'll be a lot more of *happy! Hooray!!!!*

Ridin' High

It feels so good to feel good! No…I'm not
grandiose with unrealistic expectations.
Not in a *swing* north. Steady in the
center. Just a little hyped. But a safe
hype. How nice.

What is the reason for such comfortable
feelings and mood? Just life! What?
Yeah…my life. Can't believe it. And
I'm not worrying and fearing the pleasant
state will depart. Because…I know it
WILL eventually leave.

That's what is so great about this peace.
I know it's not gonna last…and it's ok.
I'm not running, trying to make the most
of this good time in a harried way. But
I'm not taking it for granted either.

Blessed…that's what I am. Yes…I've
been blessed. For so long, a fight.
Fighting to live. Fighting to not die.
Even though I couldn't see it or feel
it, God kept a flicker of a flame lit
inside my being. Even when I would
have just a soon it be snuffed out.

What do I have to give? Give back?
Not that I feel under strain to produce
payment for just cause. No...I've
definitely already paid the price. I've
worked for this desirable state. But
the thing is...I want to share!

So, I tell you my friend. It may be dark.
So bleak. Pain...immeasurable. And go
on...it may go on and on. Undeserving.
You didn't even bring it on yourself.
But it has been your life. It just is.
Hold on. Reach out. There's help.
There will be a dawning from the misery
at hand. I ask Godspeed for you.

I take this good day...for me. And give
thanks. Thanks to God, friends, family,
dedicated and knowledgeable professionals.
Tomorrow I may not be ridin' as high.
But that's ok. Because my feet are standing
solid. Oh...I may even fall and have to
crawl. But I KNOW what can be!

To know something is attainable. That is
such security. And to know, that I as an
individual have a certain amount of
control over my destiny. No. Not All.
But enough. Just enough. And that's
all I need. So Much Gratitude.

What Is Happening?

What's happening? A change of
significance is beginning to occur.
Yes...there has been shifting,
altering and some total transformations.
But it's happening once more. Kinda
unexpected at this point.

The eyes...they are beginning to see
a different view. How's that? Well...
huh...I guess because the scene has
changed so significantly. And the
feelings that go with it. Wow!
So it's good? Believe so. At least
it looks positive at this point.

Who is this person? A disorder no
longer claims the identity. Whoa!
There's more to this life than just
survival. Nice...nice. The definition
in this person's dictionary regarding
self is changing. Oh...it has been
moving all along. But now it seems
to really be *taking off*.

No words can express detail, description
or explanation. Too vague right now.
But the sense...bordering on aura...
it is beginning to build and build.
Not to be figured out. NO! Just let
happen. Close the eyes. Remain in
the relaxed. And let it continue to
develop during a restful night of sleep.

Cake

Chains breaking. Birds flying free.
Slow breath. Heartbeat…perfect
rhythm. Head beginning to clear.
Not yet to be seen. But getting there.
Proud…not the false prideful pride.

Tension loose. Temperature just right.
Weight, no longer heavy. The ride
not weary. The forever floundering…
taking on sound gait. The audible
is smooth and enjoyable.

Wind blowing a breeze that is
refreshing and harmless. Ahh…
Notions are of the simple and easy.
Actions taken only as quiet response.
Having my cake and eating it too!
Easy…slow…easy…

Quiet Quite

I know how to spell quiet.
I know how to spell quite.
Why? Oh why do we
have to have two spellings
to one word? Of course,
they have different meanings.
But why?

Everything except the stereo
was quiet, when I tried to
spell quite. But I still didn't
get it quite right. So I sit
quietly by...while the word
quite remains hidden from
write.

Will I quietly let it go?
It is quite a bit of fuel to
the obsessive perfectionist.
I can make it be a *quiet load*,
instead of *quite a load*.
Truly, I can. So let go of the
quiet mistake. Honestly, there
is no sound. Only the repetitious
reminder that *holds no water*.
So, I will no longer give way.
And for me, that will be
quite extraordinary!

Cries Heard

Cries heard. Prayers answered. So much has been given by this gracious God. My God. The Being I talk with daily. But do I say *thank you* enough?

Cries heard. Prayers answered. You saw me when I was down. You lifted me up. Yes, you God. What can I do for you? Every day time will tell. But I know for sure...Give You Thanks.

So, Thank You my God. Thank you Father, Son and Spirit. How great is the Trinity. Access to my higher power by three different avenues. Wow! Thank you God.

Grateful. He felt my pain. Stayed with me while I struggled. He continued to hold out His hand. He said "Hang in there. I'll get you by." Through the horrors. Through the despair. Through the mind so ravaged.

In the good...let me continue to call on Him. I need you Lord. Yes, I need you in the good times. Thank you God. Thank you for the good times. When the depths are so low...the highs are higher. Not too ecstatic. Just comfortable.

So, Thank You My God. How great you are. Words such as immeasurable, infinite, stalwart, everlasting surround you...they are you. Thank you my God. Eternal Gratitude.

Daddy without Momma

We wondered. What would happen to Daddy when Momma went to heaven? Well people...It's amazing. But I kinda thought this might be the case. Some said justly...he wouldn't last long without his love. And for many spouses, the death of their beloved beckons that they follow. But not Daddy...and I'm not surprised.

Momma and Daddy...so close, intertwined, devoted, one unit. Thing is...they had a life before their life together. Daddy was 26 years old when they married... and Momma 23. See, they were the old maid and old bachelor of their hometown. Their courting didn't begin until a year before their marriage. Being from the same town, both families knew each other. But they had separate paths. Each had at least three years of college. They had worked in different cities and towns. Daddy had served 2 years in the Army. So they had lived the single life, each on their own.

So, what's happened since Momma died? Well, Daddy is more relaxed, more at ease. He's no longer suspicious and worried. He was always concerned that Momma wasn't receiving the best care. And of course, for his love...everyone and everything fell short. Even when it was optimal. Because he was the one who had always given her the perfect care. His responsibility *taken over* by strangers.

Now he can laugh. We hardly argue. See...it was somewhat my fault that they were in the nursing home...in his thoughts. He had no one easier to express blame towards...than me. But now, we joke. We remember fondly. We watch Razorback ballgames without tension between us! The amount of tenseness just depends on the score! Hahaha. He respects me... something that had been sorely missing. But it wasn't his fault. It was life...and the beginning of death...for Momma, for him.

Momma took the first step into the afterlife. And he saw that it was ok. She was out of pain...made whole again. Her funeral was not sad. We actually helped *lift her* to heaven. He had already let her go. He just needed her to go be with the Father, for him to have peace and relief.

So we take it one day at a time. Enjoy each other's company. Get on each other's nerves ever so often. Thank each other verbally. And Appreciate What Is.

Out Of Me

I want to be somewhere. But I do
like where I'm at. Things are good.
So much better than ever before.
Never dreamed it could be what
it is. It was. It is. What can it be?

What do I want it to be? Hmmm.
Well, I do know I want it to be free.
Yes...so much freedom already.
Ropes that bound...now loosened
and dropped by the wayside.

Once waving a flag, hoping to survive.
Now, sitting safe and sound. There
are ups and downs...everyday life.
But such consistency...wonderful.
A rattled, fragmented, distorted
mind-set...now a pure steady stream
of uncomplicated thought. Wow.

Where do I go from here? Oh my...
I have a choice!! That's new. Previously
my being walked on a leash, that a
hideous brain wave held tight in its
grip. And now, I can go in any direction
I so desire...with ease.

So what's up? What am I gettin' at?
Being better. Growing. Living higher.
Up until now, the act of *holding on*
caused one dimensional considerations.
And it was all inside. In me. All about me.
Selfish? Well...yeah. Just had to account
for my irrational fears and other crap.

Oh...I still want to hold onto and be
my person. But I really want to try
being out of me. Not always checking
the temperature of my body's thermometer.
No longer noting what's *coming and going*
all the time. Yes, more freedom...but not
irresponsibility.

This talk...these thoughts of not thinking...
well, they are vague. And that's alright.
Because now I don't have to have everything
solved immediately. Relaxed state. Oh...
I guess all this write might sound like a lot of
bullshit. But no...I think there's something
of relevance.

My surroundings. My brothers. The world.
They are not boxed in my mind. They are out.
Maybe...maybe it's kinda like I don't want to
be the center of my attention any longer.
No...Don't want to neglect, disrespect or lose
me. Just don't want to always be taking
my vital signs.

What's the deal? Mark the discovery.
This it may be...There is more to life...
when I can be Out of Me.

Solitaire

To put into words. I like to do that.
But sometimes...they dance around
and dart away before I can write.
Looking for a description to the *feel*.
Surely...surely...hmmm.

It's a window. Well, let's say it's one
of several windows in my mind.
All except this one opens and closes
fairly easy...for the most part.
This one seems to have been stuck
for a long time. I think it has been
opened before...but it was years ago.

Tonight I sat playing solitaire.
My train of thought was driven by
Diamonds, Clubs, Spades and Hearts.
In this freelance of processing...
a thought...or a *feel* of a thought
drifted through my mind. It did not
stay long. And I can't readily reclaim.

So, back to the window. That stuck
window slightly cracked open...and
lifted a bit. Yes, the paint that held
a seal…splintered off a speck. There
was a loosening...and the window raised
about two inches.

The two inch space...it's still there.
The window is now open. And the
feel holds so much hope. I only
felt the *feel* for brief seconds. But
there is an established promise.
Can't make be...more than is...
So, shuffle the cards and continue to
play the game.

Discomfortable

Crazy, strange...and basically amazing. What's that? How I can transform discomfort into eerie. Good Lord! Enough is enough is enough.

I'm trying to not be wrapped up in my being so much. But tonight it's been a struggle. Oh...nothing's really wrong. Fact...physically I don't feel on top of the world. But I don't feel bad. So forget any ailments as cause for the *not right*.

But back to how I can let *dis ease* evolve into eerie. Man...I've experienced some pretty eerie feelings in my life. I could put them into words right now... but I think not. No... Don't want to get deeper into shit...or should I say *go down the road to despair*. Heavens No!

GET BACK!!!! Just as I've expressed myself in these few words, relief is arriving to the scene! Wow! If anyone ever minimizes the positive properties of purging...tell them to talk to me! Right now, I feel like I've taken all my inside **gunk** and just tossed it into this brief write.

What to do now? Well...brush my teeth and go to bed. Goodnight.

Talkin' bout the Olympics

So, it's the Winter Olympics. I would bet most kids in athletics had some dreams of being in the Olympics. Of course, for me it was the Summer Olympics. No snow in Beaumont. Home of my childhood heroine Babe Didrikson Zaharias...Olympian and professional golfer. Of course, she excelled in many other sports. Anyhoo... The story I'm about to tell...I wish were only a *tale*. But it's not...it's true. *Lordy Mercy*. Here goes...

I was in college at Lamar University. My major was Physical Education...so I was somewhat athletic. Played organized basketball in junior high and high school. And was involved in a variety of other sports throughout my youth. Even though I was a fairly good basketball player, I had always just *played by the seat of my pants*. Instinctively...based on *pickup games*. There was no way THIS mind could execute formal plays. Too much junk goin' on in the head! Anyway, I was in college...and it was about a year and a half after I had begun receiving psychiatric treatment. So, I was out of dark, dark depths. Still in the depths...just not dark, dark. I was starting to be a part of life. And I decided I wanted to go a step further in my athletic ambitions. This doesn't sound good at this point...does it?? No. Just wait.

Ok. So, I had always thought it would be a great thing to be a high jumper in track and field. Yes. I stand

5'3". Medium body build. NOT tall and slender. BUT I thought...why not? What??? Yep. For several weeks my mind entertained the thought of being a collegiate high jumper. Now, I would not experience *official* manic episodes until my 30's. But uh. Hmmm. Not lookin' good...is it? Yes. I will be a high jumper for Lamar University. WHAT THU HELL???? I had never even participated in track and field...except the public school Presidential Physical Fitness Award stuff. Remember that? (Yes, Melissa...I know you do!) Anyway. But I was a jogger and in good physical shape. Why not? Really?? Ugh...

So, one day I find myself in the Lamar track coach...*the head track coach's* office. OH MY GOD!!!!! I explained to him, that I felt as though I wanted to try out for being a high jumper on the school team. Of course, he asked about my experience with the sport. I told him I had never attempted to high jump, but I'd like to try and I thought I'd be good at it. OH LORD NO!!!!!!!!!! HIDE NOW!!!!!! At this point I must interject...I don't think you have to be manic to have a break with reality. What's that called? Psychosis? Lord help me!!!!! Well, anyway he was kind...I'm sure he was thinkin' where in the hell did this girl come from? He told me they were having their first practice of the season in a couple of days...and come and try out. I said ok. HOLD ON... it doesn't get That Bad. He also told me that all the women athletes were having a meeting in the women's gym the next day. Kinda an orientation of sorts. He told me I should attend.

Well, I went to the women athletes meeting. I saw my high school buddy there. She was on Lamar's tennis team. I'm sure in her mind...when I told her why I was there...she probably thought...SHE'S CRAZY!!!!!! What's gone wrong with her???!!!! But she was kind too. (There's something about when people are *kind* to you...in these situations. They are actually wanting to scream in your face...YOU'RE NUTS!!!! But they don't. They are *kind*.) Her response to my fabricated aspirations in track and field, was to encourage me to try out for the women's basketball team. Nope. Don't want to do that. I knew at that point...somehow I had logical reasoning that I could not *carry out* basketball plays. So, no to basketball. Then she suggested cross country. Yes. I was a runner. But honestly...more of a jogger. And I knew my limits there. So, no...Don't want to run long distance. Given those two reasonable assessments of my athletic capabilities, WHY IN THE HELL DID I THINK I COULD BE A HIGH JUMPER... OUT OF THE BLUE?????? The answer...Hell if I know. So, I left the women's meeting with my mind still in the direction of high jumping. (Thanks for trying Cheryl!)

THERE'S GOOD NEWS!!! However it happened... sometime in the next couple days... I slowly kinda thought...you know, I probably need to have had some experience in high jumping before I *try out* for the college track and field team. WHEW!!!!!!!!!!!!!! Reality...It can be a very good thing. HELL NO!!!! It was a GREAT THING!!!!!! Saved me from Total Humiliation! God help me!!! HE DID!!! Hahaha. No.

It was like the *drive* to be a high jumper seemed to be put into perspective in a period of two days. THANK YOU LORD!!!!!!!!!!!!! (For some reason I can hear a lot of laughter right now.) Anyhoo...

So, back to the Olympics. Well, during the time that I had my mind geared towards being a collegiate high jumper... I was also *seeing myself* participating in the Summer Olympics!!! WHAT THU??? Yes...an Olympic High Jump Medalists. "THE GOLD" of course!!!! What else??

People...I don't understand all the *absolutes* about psychiatric disorders. Why we have them. How they happen. I just know for a couple of weeks during my college years, I definitely had delusions of grandeur!!! Ya Think?? You know...for some reason God saw fit that I didn't hold embarrassing shame about that incident. BUT at the same time...I never thought I'd write about it!!! Hope you got a good laugh!!

No Poles

It's a groove. Comfortable. Satisfying.
Neither hot nor cold. In between t-shirts
and sweaters. Just right. A combination
of spring and fall. Easy swaying.

Volume of sound, just a tad above medium.
There's a beat. Perfect rhythm. Nothing
stark. Sight not strained or blurred.
Contrast doesn't determine the affect.
Internal drive and being, on a stable
cruise control. Energy glides easily.

Far from being hard. But not too soft.
A solid tenderness. The soul is moved
only by the security of unrehearsed calm.
No seeking. And not hiding. To be.
Just to be. Being Blessed.

From Here

Where do we go from here?
Or should I say...Where do I
go from here? Talking, writing,
contemplating...all taking a turn.
Oh my...the future. What's to be?

You! Did I ever tell you that you
are special? You heard. You read.
You listened. You responded.
Yes. Thank you. You let me enter
into your mind. And hopefully, also
your heart and soul. My friend.

I want it to be good. Good for you.
Good for me. Definite to be ups
and downs. But overall...a stabilizing
sense is the goal. At least for me.
I hope you to be as fortunate as me.
We can have it. A solid appreciation.

What do you need? What do you want?
Help? *Do you need a hand?* What
can I do for you? How can I make your
world better? It's about you. You
deserve good. Security, love, fun...
yes...you should have. And happy.

Tonight I give you my prayer. That is all I know to do…tonight. For all the souls that read…I pray blessings and peace. May you have restful sleep. Resume the walk of life tomorrow.
We can walk side by side…
With God as our guide. Tranquility.

What Can One Be?

Professions, careers, jobs, odd jobs.
What to do? Why are we here?
What is the purpose? For so long…
no beneficial pattern to follow.
Gettin' by. The best to hope for.

A purpose in life…we all want.
So far out of reach. Survival the
only method of living. Reasons
to breathe, share, care…at a loss.
Goals? Ha! Only for the lucky.

How did the gap get bridged?
Working, striving, suffering, learning.
Hold on…Hold on…Kept holding on.
The grasp of what is still somewhat
of an aura…is getting tighter. And
it's good! Thanks to the Higher Realm.

At one point…it was severely tested.
Purpose…that is. Alone in a mind
of conflict, turmoil and pain. Such
fear abounded. So what did this one
claim as reason for life? Searching.
Reaching. What can I do? What is
my purpose in life? From above an
answer was clear…
"Be nice to people." And it all made sense.

Looking Outward

To hear. To sense. To see.
The eyes of the soul have
turned...and now the view is
of the world. The being no
longer bound to self-absorbed
survival. No guilt. It's what
it was. Could be no different
at the time.

How times have changed! Yes!!
So looking outward...what is
seen? Brothers and sisters. Some
hurting. Some healed. No doubt,
hurt and heal for everyone. Everyone!
No one gets away. It's a must. Life.

Are some stuck? Can't help but be.
Times can be hard and rough.
People can be hard and rough.
You're hurting. They're hurting.
Crying among many. Wait!
There's hope. It will happen.
Not necessarily a justice. Instead...
a love. Love of God, self and neighbor.

To tease with carefree *feel-good*. Is
that the scheme, to bring a lift above
the rest of the masses? No. It's for
real. There can be peace, hope and joy.
No lie. Won't be all the time. Maybe
just now and then. But it will be
enough to make life a positive vibe.

It's not just getting a new mind-set or
stable train of thought *at the drop of a hat*.
No. It takes hard work. Tears. Fears.
But hang on. It will be. Sure as the
depths are so low...the heights will
be of the heavens. And the doves fly.

Escaping Fear

For so long...all my life...Fear.
It could suffocate, bring pain,
bolster doubts. Doubts about
everything. The here and now.
And the ever after. Especially,
the ever after. It had a chokehold
on my person, my being.

It's not that I was *trembling* all
the time. I could be sure and
certain of myself. But those times
were few. Fortunately, in the past
six or so years...the tight grip of
fear has gradually lessened.

I'm finding that I am now at a
point in which I'm starting to
look away from fear. Why?
Why in the hell keep watching
a scary movie, when I have the
natural tendency to be nerve-wracked?

So...I'm not gonna pay any attention
to fear anymore. Does this mean I
do not take note of true dangers
and *slippery slopes*? No. I can
let go of unfounded...and sometimes
founded trepidation, using common
sense. Each situation can be determined
individually.

But the **Fear Game**...that's what I'm
stepping out of. No more. It's already
starting to happen. Pretty neat! Not
really sure which direction I'm going yet.
But it is *out of*...
What's that? *It's out of myself!!!!*
Yes. Earlier today, I felt some apprehension.
And at that moment, my thought was...
It's not about me. And relief came instantly!

Honestly. If you think about it...my internal
digestive tract of the mind...It can be Spooky!
So, why stay in it? Be out of me. But I
don't like the idea that there's that *haunted
house* in my being...even if I step out of the
anxiety. Well, what to do? How to fix?
What else to do...but turn it over to God.

Yes. I've turned many things in my life
over to the care of God. And then there
have been those items which I've clenched
tightly...not that it was for my good. My
stubborn will. But I see now...I want
God to have that *haunted house* inside
of me. You can have it God. I have no
idea what you're gonna do with it. But
that's none of my business!

So, right now I've given God my *haunted house*. I don't own it anymore. I don't have to figure out how to function in it because...well, because I'm out of it. But wait...it's still inside...hmmm. Here it is! I think I'm gonna let God use His makeover skills to turn that *haunted house* into anything He so desires.

God has told me to "Fear Not." So, I'm certain His renovation is gonna be secure, light, sound, stable and at ease. It's going to be a relaxed state. Right now, I can see windows being raised and a pleasant breeze blowing fresh air for me to breathe. No longer the suffocation. Nice. And the color of the walls are being painted a nice soothing, kind color. A light shade of blue-green. Yes. That's it.

So, I'll stay out of me. It's not about me. I'm God's. I'm on this earth to be of use to Him and help others. Oh...sure, I'll look out for myself...but it will be *out of myself*. It's not about me. Thank the Lord! It's about time!!!

Why Does There Have To Be Somethin'?

Somethin'. Something's wrong. But there's not. Everything is just fine. What to do? There's always been somethin'. And now there's not... if I do decide that there's nothin'.

So, it's a choice. There can be somethin' or there can be nothin'. What if it's nothin'? I mean...What do I do if there is nothin'? And when I say "nothin'"...I mean there's nothing wrong. Right or wrong. Wrong or right. Nothing to do with morality and such. But *the feel*.

The feel. Right now there's nothin' wrong with *the feel*. Stable, secure, at ease. Nice. I don't want to jinx...but it's been this way a lot lately. Not all in one succession. It can come and go. But most of the time nowadays, nothin's wrong with *the feel*. Wow.

At this moment, I'm really not too sure what to think...not that I have to think about anything. But what do I think about nothin' being wrong with *the feel*? Hmmm.

Think I'll just let *things* float. Yes.
That's it. I'm on an inner tube down
at the creek. A rope attached securely
to the tube...the other end of the rope,
wrapped tightly around a big rock.
And that rock is not moving an inch.

I'm safe and sound...just floating.
When it's time to get out of the water
and do somethin' else, then I'll make
a move. Right now, just float and do
nothin'. Because there's nothin' to
make into somethin'.

Swirling Words

So, I'm at a point of *even keel*.
Yay! Never expected this to
happen. Actually, I had no tangible
reference that it could even be.

Now that I'm here...it's nice. But
I do want motion. I want to go
forward. Not fast. Not hurried.
Not because I have to move out of fear.
But because I want to be better.

Do I think I'm *not good enough*?
No, no. That's old-timey thinking.
At least my old way of thinking.
What's that? My old way of thinking
is that the opposite of *better* is
not good enough.

I want to be *better* in and of itself.
Always striving to be the best...is the
way to constantly be moving towards
better. It's a sure thing. Production.
Climb mountains? Swim rivers?
Win the game? Not necessarily.

Speaking of *to be*. Be the best I
can be at *being*. And that does
include movement. Movement in
a positive direction.

So, I'm at a wonderful *to be*. Yes.
So nice. Relax, enjoy, *take it all in*.
Ok. But making plans. Formulating
in my mind a bit. I do want to make
my life better. It's so great that I'm
wanting to be better...and it's not out
of desperation or survival.

What is it then? It's enhancement!
Yes. I want to enhance my life.
I want to enhance my *being*.
Well...what do I do? Not sure yet.
Go to bed and see what tomorrow brings.

Why Not?

Does there have to be an answer when
someone ask *why not?* Hmmm.
Should I have just wrote...
Does there have to be an answer when
someone ask *why not??*
Well...Anyway...

Does everything have to make sense
or feel right before we *make a move*?
I'm guessing No! If that were the
case...then a lot would never happen.
A lot of what? A lot of what we want
or need to happen.

So...there are times that we just *do*.
Without even letting our minds past
the question mark of *why not?*
Oh...if only so simple. But really, if
we take the dissection of *why not?*
to the extreme...it truly is easy!

I'm going no further in this write.
There is an issue of which I'm
asking myself *Why not?* It
involves changing a behavior.
If I delve deeper...it will negate
the simplicity of *why not?*

I just told a friend that I didn't want to *shoot myself in the foot* for *shooting myself in the foot*. She said... "No...Because it would cause a hole." Very True.

My Definition

People would always say, with kinda an air of authority/superiority...*Don't let your disability define you.* Well, fine. But what if that's all you've known? Shit. Oh...yes, I had other aspects to my life that had *life*. But they always paled in importance as they *sat beside* my mental disorders. Since survival of some sort was at stake so much of the time, my disorders demanded a lot of my attention and respect. They were actually a type of thief. Thank God for progress!

So, I'm a female. I'm a daughter. I'm a sister. I'm an aunt. I'm a cousin. Ok. Well...hmmm. I could say I'm a college graduate. But does that define? Oh...I know, it's a part of me. But really people...what if you don't have a lot going for you? How do you present yourself to the world? It's hard. Introductory conversations are *hard to hold* when you don't have some sort of springboard. One of the first questions...*What do you do?* Uh. Well... I answered that question during my life in many different ways. Whatever I could grab ahold of and hang onto at that point in my life. For instance, I would be doin' good if I had a recent odd job. "Oh, right now I'm just detailing cars and doing various jobs for my friend's used car lot." That's about as good as it got for most of my life. And if someone would ask me the same question two months later...I was at a loss. So...don't let my disorder define me? Huh. How do my bills get paid? I get a check deposited into my bank account every month. The end. It's hard people! People want to know *what you're about*. And what can be said? Again...it's a bunch of finagling. And in the end, if the conversation goes anywhere... *you're found out*. Yes...the true you. The disorders. Now, I always knew I was more than a disorder...but what to say? Well, enough. You get the point.

Now. Nowadays. How do I define myself? Gladly, I can say I've progressed. True...if I am asked...*What do you do?* My answer...*I'm on disability*. So, it's still a concession of sorts. But it's different now. How so? BECAUSE...It's Not Who I Am! YAY! I have mental disorders...but they are not me. My perception of self has changed...grown. So, what am I? Ok. We got the basics...female, daughter, etc...We got that down. But to go further. No...Not a mother, grandmother, wife, partner. Well...hmmm. How do I define myself? Well, at this moment I just know this... I am on this earth to do what God wants me to do...and to help other people. And really, that is a sufficient definition. And it's nice that I can say I graduated from Lamar University in 1986 and recently published a book. *That's where I'm at*. Good enough!

See The Stain

The other day I made a coat.
It is attractive, comfortable and warm.
Made with strong material, it can
resist water and stretch when needed.
Very durable fabric. Yes, indeed.

Like every garment...it has its own
style. Some are fond of the colors
and design...desiring the piece.
Others are looking for something
different to wear. My coat is not
for them. And that's ok.

I can make numerous replicas from the
pattern. In fact, it's exciting to share
the *feel*. The pleasing sense that the
article can present. Just one thing...
there is a stain that can't be removed...
even in reproduction. Damn!

Is the coat any less warm because of
the stain? No. Is the coat any less
comfortable because of the stain? No.
Does the stain make for an eyesore?
It depends on the eye of the beholder.
So, it may bother some...and others
could care less of the imperfection.

So, I have a coat I want to give. It
provides so much protection from
the elements. It has brought enjoyment
and delight to a good number who
have worn it. But it has a small stain.

The stain is from the same color family
as the coat. So it's not glaring and
outstanding. Yet, it exists. It's located
next to one of the button holes. Honestly,
when someone is wearing the coat...the
stain is the last thing on their mind.

So, am I gonna continue to cringe at
the stain? I mean the garment has been
beneficial to many people...and could
continue to make more people suited
for inclement weather. Does that stain
take from its worth? Hell No!

That's It People! The imperfection has
no effect on the *worth* of the coat. Yes...
the coat is *worthy* to be worn. More
than that...it is desired by some. So, will
I continue to cringe? Well, what's seen
can't be unseen. A given. To accept! Ah!

Yes. I have to accept that I made a coat
that has a small stain on it. Again...the coat
can keep the individual warm and comfortable.
And the coat is attractive, regardless of the

slight visual imperfection. No...No effect on its worth. It is a worthwhile piece of clothing and a worthwhile work of art.

Me to myself: *Just continue to sew.*

A Circus

In a barrel, swirling all around.
Talk. Chatter. Laugh. Loud!
Time passes in slow motion.
And the movement is not felt.
Not necessarily numb...
just oblivious.

So, bad? No...Not at all. In fact,
trying to not be too good.
Well...you know...mania. Wait.
That's not what it is. It's just a
damn good hyper!!!

So doors open and close, while
the mouth opens and closes.
People come and go. And the
voice is a constant flow. Kinda
radical at times. But Fun! Or
so it is for the one talking.
Probably hard on listening ears.
But what the heck!

Oh...others are laughing too.
Laughing at the topic and the
subject. And if they're game...
they become a part of the circus.
A fun time. A funny time.
A silly fling of an evening, which
holds relevance to nothing pertinent.

I'm tired! I'm worn out. Nobody is hurt. No bad decisions. Ain't life GOOD!!!!!

Better?

All this talk of moving forward.
Yes, life in positive motion.
Well...huh. I don't know. I talk
of wanting to be better...and the
best that I can be. But do I really
want to put forth the effort. Man...
I sound lazy. I'm not denying.
And I'm not in denial. So let's face it.

What to do to be better? Well, as
far as my *person*...my *physical
person*...I'm a Ragamuffin!!!
Oh my. And my education and
studies revolved around body fitness.
Yes. I could do with exercise and
healthy nutrition. And a *fit body*
usually involves making the most
of physical appearance. Well, folks...
I'm miles away from such destination.

Now, I know being a *better person*
does not necessarily involve outward
looks...but for the sake of this writing,
we're gonna let it be the focal point.
God help me! I'm in deep.
No, no. I'm not committing myself
to a *makeover*...yet.

So, do I want to look like one of those children on cold city streets during the times of Charles Dickens? You know... coal marks on my face. Or to bring it up to date...Do I want to be the *Poster Person* depicting a Walmart customer? Not *downing* Wally World. I shop there. But you know the stereotype... shopping in pajamas.

Considering being a better person, includes making the most of my looks and my health. UGH!!!! Don't want to put forth the effort. Not in a depressed sense. More like...I don't want to be bothered. It's not a priority. It's beginning to sound a lot like lazy!

Ok. So I'm a bum when it comes to the issue at hand...looking like an attractive member of society. Yes. I'm a lowlife in that regard. What am I gonna do about it? Am I *gonna* do anything about it? Do I want to do anything about it? Well...not at this moment. Hmmm. Some consolation... as to ignore responsibility. I'm saving money on soap, shampoo, electricity and laundry detergent. That's NOT consolation... THAT'S BULL!!!!!

Well...this write has not proclaimed any new revelation. No forward movement. So for tonight...I'll just...just...I'll just... What's that? I'll Just Be Lazy!!!!!

Out Of A Problem

What do I get out of a problem?
Really? Have I become so well?
Actually, things are going my way.
Thankfully, sense is being made
of this one time very distraught life.

So, I don't have any problems? Well...
no. Well, yeah...actually. Considering
my past...I have absolutely no
problems at the present moment.
Should I be so extreme in such a
statement? Well, just play along...

My life used to be hell. Now I'm
at peace. So, I'm using that as the
measuring stick. New waters.
Unfamiliar territory. Not sure what
to expect. So, look for or make up
a problem so I'll feel comfortable?
GOD HELP!!!!! Haha It's so true!

Now, if I do conjure up an issue into
a *problem*...it's usually not obvious
until after the fact. So....goin' kinda
blindly into crap. Just so I'll feel
safe and sound in chaos, remorse,
guilt and low self-esteem. My, oh my.

What can I call something I want to change...but I'm having an extremely hard time changing? I'm not gonna call it a *problem* anymore. Nope. Because on my scale of relevant problems...it bottoms out.

Really? Does it have to have a name?! Shoot. Giving it more validity than it deserves...setting it up to go into the direction of becoming a *true problem*. No. No name. Enter the powerful world of obsessive-compulsive.
No Thank You!!!

So there's something I want to change... but I don't want to...what's that? I don't want to do what it takes to change. Well... just sit in the mire! Ok.
At least I'm not making it into a *problem*! YAY!!!!! (Ahh...a bit of progress!)

Neutral

Not forward...not backward.
Neither right nor left.
Definitely not a matter of
right or wrong. Well...
that fact is a nice change
of existence.

Not reviewing the past.
As for the future...kinda
drawing a blank. But there's
not an obsessive fascination
as to where paths will lead.
Just sitting in neutral.

Thoughts on several goals.
But action not yet to be taken.
That's fine. This is where I
need to be. Sometimes a bit
of tease on the mind. More
often totally comfortable.

Some apprehension can creep
up...until I clarify. Clarify what?
My next move. Not so fast.
Unknown future a must for this one.
Sit and idle in neutral for the time being.
When it's time to drive...make sure
God is in the driver's seat.
Then just Cruise!

Why Moves

The motion of *why*. It varies, depending on consequences and relevance to its reasoning. Shifting up and down, bringing chaos and continued unknown. In fact, with more question...the *why* is embellished.

Oh, to accentuate one's intelligence...*why* is thought to be larger than life. To the seeker and those who find. Spread the news...we have the answer! No. Not quite. Forever elusive. *Why* is always open-ended. Forever...

What about the *feel* of lack of definition? Scary? Frightful? Apprehensive? A shadiness of sacrilege settles around the honest *why*. Why? Because there are to be absolutes. God forbid the thought of unknown to what has become substance of breath.

Why moves. Will it destroy? Only if there is an insistence for the question to be fully answered. Let go. It's alright. Peace can be attained while *why* bounces back and forth, and in and out of light. There doesn't have to be certain darkness with *why* unresolved.

So to function among the blur of *why*?
Take the next step. Do the best thing.
Treat as one wants to be treated. Care.
Walk, talk, share. Be among others to their
best interest. There is more to life...and there
is life...even when *why* is but a drifting
obstacle to purpose. *Because*...God knows.

Blind Mind

So I'm stuck. Well, what's new?!
What's really happening? This...
I'm not allowing myself to be the
best that I can be. Wait a minute.
I thought I was gonna be *out of me*.
Oh...I still am. It's just a little adjustment.
And very necessary.

I wonder how much of my lack of
discipline is related to my Obsessive-
Compulsive Disorder? Strange...
I think there is a lot to the disorder that
goes about wreaking havoc...in disguise.
We all get a clear picture of the usual
obsessive-compulsive behaviors. And for
many...many are just now realizing how
obsessive-compulsive thinking can totally
control a person's *insides*. Not visual to
others. The person goes it alone in every
respect.

At this point, I look at what I've just wrote...
and yes, *it's all about me*. Ugh. Don't want
to stay here. And won't! But got to figure.
Really? Do I have to figure it out? Well...
things need to change...and that takes some
understanding. Doesn't it? Or do I *just do it*?
That has never been one of my strong points...

to *just do it*. So...I find it hard to *just do it*.
And at the same time, I don't want to make that
fact an *official problem*. Damn. Giving it
more power. Damn. Trying to diffuse not increase.

Wait! No progress with write. Baby steps.
Tomorrow morning I'll call my friend...
we'll meet and walk...as planned. Let it go.

Minus Torment

How do you live when you're not surviving?
Things are good. Real good. Oh...there
are days...and moments. But overall, life's
a breeze...well, compared. No deep lows.
No extreme highs. Balanced and stable.
So much for which to be thankful. And yes...
I am very grateful.

But what do I do? Well, *I'm caregiving*.
And when the spirit moves, I write words.
I have some responsibilities to others and
myself. But it's odd. It's strange and different
not to be battling torment. Oh yeah...I can get
used to it. And I am. It's just...now I need
to take the next step.

On the outside, one would probably say I'm
a bit depressed. But on my insides I'm so
relaxed. You see...depression to me means
dark, black, terror. Now I have to get associated
with average depression. Hmmm. What a kick!
A lull. No fight. Mild lethargy. But so comfortable.
Compared to...

Do you know how enjoyable it is to just sit?
To just be in one spot and there is no pain.
No rattled brain. No chaos. No friction in my
mind. I could just sit and sit. And enjoy and
enjoy. And I Have! Again...there have been
moments of fragility. But with the rebound…
all the more joy. So, now where?

Honestly, I do not have a clear picture of
what my future might hold. I kinda have a
view of what is sure to be. You know...deaths
and life. The meaning of life and all thereabouts.
Got that covered. Feels pretty good. Sound and
solid. But my everyday...every day. Don't know.
I don't have anything else for this write...because
it is where I am. Wherever that is. Which is here.
How comforting. Truly.

Forever Highway

It's a long straight haul. And yet
continuously going in circles.
The rain drizzles, as wheels travel
a well-worn path. Where to? To
find. To find it.

Never *just out of reach*. No, never
that close. Longed for...a lifetime.
Not constantly...but once again the
stretch of highway is paced. The
destination is never secure. In fact,
it isn't even solid. Never tangible.

Meeting oncoming traffic. Wonder
if they know where they're are going?
Do they ever get there? This ride...
early on...occasional passengers. But
for many years the venture is by oneself.

Not many traffic lights. And definitely
no true direction. Sometimes speeding.
Sometimes taking time...to take up time.
Dreams in music. Music a pure steady
beat. Loud. Over and over the lyrics.
Known for so long. Again and again.
Hits every sense. Reminders. Wishes.

The return trip...as always leads to
where the ride began. No progress made.
Rides in the dark. Who are they for?
Some feel it is their lot in life. This one
has driven and driven. Earlier...assumed
the trip had to produce. Then realized
it didn't have to be definite. And that's ok.

But every once in awhile, the road is
travelled. Someday. Maybe one day.
Could it be? If it isn't...it's alright.
Ride to ride. Ride to dream. Ride to
wish. Ride to see headlights shining
through the windshield. Ride to get
the feel of what could be. Who knows?
Just another motion of life.

High School Radio

A night ends the day. Tunes breathe
an imagined friend. The clock radio
so beloved, as the timer is reset to
play more magic. Into the dark,
songs flow with every sensation of
what could be...perhaps tomorrow.

The hustle and bustle of everyday
studies. Room to room. Peers that
give and take. Laughter, fear, fun,
embarrassment and all emotions...
on and off the wall. *Our* music spills
over the loudspeaker as we eat. Feelings
and thoughts we dare to understand.
Ahh...how about the beat?!

Ridin' the drag. The best! Music moves...
literally. The latest and loudest hits sound
from the station of choice. Usually...the same
all in one...even when we think so unique.
Friends and talk explode into a world of
what we hope will be the prospect of the
next weekend. We keep dreamin' of that day.

Will we get the chance? To sway in darkness
with a special other. After the game. At the
end of the year. Sometime. Please, at least
one dance. We can only hope.

The songs of our youth...
Forever with us. They are us. We make them
be the sound of our heart and reasoning, from
a time...that was both happy and sad. To this
day, the power of our music can simply stir
or totally ignite a force. Leading us to feel
what was or wasn't. Mellow, soft, hard, rough...
Whatever the groove...Get Down!

Layer Of Dread

I guess it's been there all along.
A layer. Just below the surface.
Probably years earlier it settled
deeper. But due to all my *gardening*,
it is being cultivated out. I hope.

This layer...it can cause immediate
failure or fault to occur internally.
The emotion involved resembles a type
of doom. Not a destructive doom in the
sense that the catastrophe would bring harm.
No. Just a dread.

This dread...it keeps things from being
settled, peaceful, realistic, positive.
It is a black or white thing. You know...
either or. It is not limited to one aspect
of my life. There is not one particular
topic, subject or situation that brings it
on. It just happens in a generalized sense.

Let's say I'm just sitting and thinking
of what I have to do the next day. I'll
consider the task at hand...or thought at
hand. If there is any of the least type of
conflict in my analysis...an emotion
immediately *kicks in*. Kinda like it is
an inevitable burden to bear. No middle
ground. From comfortable to uncomfortable.

Like a misfiring of thought processes. Hmmm. That would be appropriate given my makeup. Ya think?! Hahaha. I don't know...but just the realization tonight of this *faulty wiring* is already taking some of its potency away. Wow! And I continue to Break Free!!!!
Thank you God.

What Can Be?

What can be? Living in this aura of luxury. Bare mind games. *Playing field* even with self. No longer an opponent within. There does not have to be an ongoing strategy to overcome desperation.

What can be? Peace. Yes. Peace. The process complete? No. Not at all. Never the finish line, until last breath. So, one could say a goal in life is to *keep the peace coming!* Reality. There will be down days. For sure. But now one knows if peace leaves, it can surely return.

So when peace is hangin' around... Leave It Alone. Don't complicate. Don't analyze. Don't look for *the reason for*. Let it settle into every corner and crevice of the brain waves. Let it flourish. If anything...encourage it. How so? Know it is deserved. Accept. Continue to breathe and say a prayer of thanks. Let God Be Great!

A Second Mind

When the mind doesn't work, it's
good to have a second mind.
When the mind works, it's good
to have a second mind.

I have a second mind. It cooks and
cleans. It is multi-tasked. It is kind
and funny. It makes my first mind
think with a different perspective.

My second mind listens very carefully.
My second mind considers my feelings.
My second mind challenges me.
My second mind gives credit where
credit is due.

Ha. How about that! Not long ago I
despised having a *single* mind. It
was all I could handle. AND I didn't
handle it very well. Thing is...this
second mind is complementing what
is transforming from my original mind.

So, with all that has been said...one
might think this write is a bunch of
hogwash. No. It's for real. It's a real
mind. It's a real person. And it really,
really is a true friend! Thank you K.

Cousin

He's small town. Could've been farm bound.
His words he picks and strums. Sometimes
smooth, sometimes coarse. Love and pain
weave in and out of each verse. So much
inside waiting to evolve into a melody,
only some can handle. Oh yes...you can
hear. But can you feel?

His intellect obvious to those who listen.
Schooled, taught, learned. Skilled to prepare
what your soul left on this earth...to rest
in peace. He has given his name to *special
three*. Sense of humor dry, sometimes
sacrilege...always funny as hell!

The mind...his enemy. As with his cousin
who writes of him. They share the burden
of genetics that force a cruel setting to
some of the best of days. Wait! Hold on!
Let life catch up, and overcome the inhumane
features of the internal grinding gears.

It can be. This world. The music. The write.
For he and cousin...let the artistic flare *fly in the
face* of the hideous side of bloodline. Let the
ticking demonic brain waves diminish as song
and words flow. Laugh at the devil! Sing.
Speak. Share the tormented insides until they
run out of the body, screaming the lyrics and
thoughts penned. Banished!

Life…it will be good. Peace…it can be afforded.
Paying the price for sanity…not always easy.
May take a while. Prayers said to an awesome
God. The day will break here on earth.
Freedom. Flight. And song and write will
be at ease. A fraction of heaven.

You Know I Know...and I probably do.

Do we all have a mask? To hide.
To hide faults, thoughts, fears.
Yes...many times too often.
Oh, how we've failed. We should
have done the opposite. The
fright inside...too fragile to expose.

What about when we know we're
screwed up? Yeah. We are *basket
cases*. Dare to enter: *What can we
get by with*? Really? Are we
so smothered by our emotional
state that we venture to play the
intentional or unintentional victim?

So you think you're alone. The only
one who has traveled this road. Pain,
loss, fear, threats to reality. Surely
no other has encountered so many
harsh elements. No one truly and
honestly understands how the mind
mistreats you. No way. They can't.

To live among features of your person
that have less than complimentary
results. You're getting by. Day by day.
One day at a time. Right? Yeah.
As long as you can keep your head
above water.

What if you want more? Familiar words
from my past: *I'll share just enough
for notice... I'm answering your question
but you don't understand... I'm different,
in a way... It's not the same with me...
I've already tried that method... It doesn't
work for me... We're not alike...*

How long can it go on? How long do
you want to live in a world, of which
you are both resident and visitor?
You can *have your cake and eat it too.*
You think? Keep ostracizing. Cling to
the false pride which keeps you in a life
of comfortable solitary confinement.
Comfortable... being familiar and safe...
or so you assume.

And you think nobody knows. Hell!
We all wrote the damn book!!!!!
We're in it together. If given a chance,
we can relate in one fashion or another.
Dare to think something different.
Listen to what another says...and take
into consideration it may be correct.
Let someone in. Ugh. Show your
true colors...yes, the shades of your
affection.

You know I know, because I've taken
the same exact path to avoid living
among mankind. There's no fooling
the fool. And foolish it was, to think
that I could survive without holding
the hand of another.

So I squirmed and wallowed in my sole
person until I Wanted More. And then
I conceded. Yes. You understood my
conflict, hurts and longings. You've
clung to desperation as the only force
to ensure life. I saw that you saw me.
You knew me, and I knew you knew me.
The game was over. I took off the mask.

The world welcomed me. And I have to
play my part. I have to give and receive.
Live and let live. Love. Share. Not only
play my part...but be a part. What magnificent
colors appear, in the delightful kaleidoscope
of humanity. *I bought in. Won't you?*

Come So Far

Come so far. From there to here.
There could be deep and dark.
Or maybe more like a rushed
vacuum...with consequences
that deterred stable living.
Greater than deterred...demolished.

Then *there* was *just getting by*...
with some very good days. Well...
compared to the original *there*.
A lot accomplished during that
span. Things of which to be proud.
Some fun. Some life.

There were times of which
seemed to be backtracking or
shooting self in foot. But it never
really was an about-face going
backward. It was more like stalled
in a mess that had to be owned.

There was paying dues for the
privilege...or not...of holding status
of too much insight. Really? Yeah.
Way too much insight. Ya know...
incessant, internal evaluating. Leading
to a self-consuming theory of the
reason why. Always of the negative.

At times *there* really *stepped it up*.
So much better than it had been.
True progress. Relief from semi-misery.
Fortunately, the blindsided misery
had been reduced to half. Really...more than
half...more like total overhaul of the
psyche. And yet...half misery remained?
At least that's how I see it from *here*.

Here. How about *here*? It's really
nice to be *here*. It's safe and relaxed.
I can let go *here*. I can let be *here*.
Here is kind to me. Others enjoy
being around *here*. And those others
are enjoyed *here*.

Where is *here*? It is life as I now
know it. Satisfaction and comfort are
always lingering. In a split second,
negative can become positive *here*.
God is gentle *here*. Easier to trust.
That's it! Think I'll stay *here*.
Grateful.

LoveLife

It first started when learned
there could be soul for soul.
Another to light and stir,
causing intensity to heighten
with the loss of words.

When younger, dreaming of the
cutest fox. Always reaching for the
cream of the crop of looks. Regardless
the league in which self is categorized.
Labels. Hmmm… Oh well…
The cover of a magazine.

Place of the *social* solid. Now
look for compatibility…with some
fineness. Has to be some features
that start the chemistry. Of course.
But no longer striving for G.Q.
And the songs…there was, is and
always will be *that song*.

Growing. Aging. Maturing.
Facing and accepting reality of
identity and relations. But still
the hunt continues…just a bit
different. A bit? Ya think? Hahaha
Laugh at life!

Still there's the appeal of what's
out of reach. Why not? Reach
for the stars. The movie stars...
sometimes. So the mind teases.
Who says what can't be? Really?
Get real.

Next stage finds the earth. You know,
get down to earth. Oh yes...things in
common. Goals that can coexist.
Or at least that sounds good...to the
naïve thirty-something trying and
trying to find *the one*.

Going it alone in the forties...
for all practical purposes. Intent on
surviving for the best of days. The
onset of fifties brought new perspective.
Set in ways. Not to move...too much.
Just company. Just a companion.
But enough charisma to bring a twinkle
to the eyes...and secure a passion.

So, how's it goin'? Well...a loner.
But not sad. Don't feel cheated. Lovin'
life as it is. In fact, life is really, really
good. Being blessed. Hell! Only chance
to be taken...is when there is a stamp
on the forehead saying "God Approved!"
No...not gonna mess up things. All the
while, holding sacred special memories.
And every now and then play *that song*.

Let Freedom Ring

The links in the chains broken.
Masks are removed. A smile on
the face and in the heart. What
was once an undermining affair
with the mind...now just a walk,
hand in hand with the soul.
Let Freedom Ring.

How can it be? Such change with
regard to how one views their person.
Heartache, heartbreak...not from
circumstance involving others...
but from a tyrannical brain. It has
been squelched. Again...how can
it be? Definitely not magic. But
an omnipotent God, true friends,
secure family, science and medicinal
wonders AND hard work. Along
with a steady dose of love.

So thanks and gratitude to resound
in the heart. And aloud to testify the
promise to and for others. Did I
tell you God is Great? Yes...He is.
Parting waters, turning water to wine,
healing lepers and casting out demons.
Casting out my demons! Oh, you say
what an overstatement. No! It's true.

Demons...we all have them. But in this mind...vanished...or if you will, ordered out by the miracles of good people and a good God.

The body has been relaxing. Every once in awhile the anxious animals return to try and play havoc. But in the end to no avail. The foundation of change is on solid ground. It can take a beating and still stand upright. Or more realistically...there may be a slight fall, but followed by a bounce back up to meet life face on.
Let Freedom Ring! Rejoice!

Now what to do? Well, let the stability and safety grow. Give appreciation in maximum volume and allowance. Continue to work for more progress in securing what has been attained. Plow, plant and reproduce what can be ongoing calm, reason and a newfound dignity. Swim into once feared waters. Yes. There is a lifeguard. Can even float on the back...Ahh...
Such ease. Must share.
Yes indeed. The bells of freedom are ringing in this life! Forever grateful.

My Jesus

Jesus, remember 1972 when I first met you?
Yes...I know you do. At that moment you
were so simple. Easy to figure. I just said
"Here I am." And you became the Lord
of my life. Thank you for making it so
easy for me to come into your world.
Because I know it was a hard price for
you. The whole thing is amazing.
Yep. Amazing Grace.

Jesus, you know that I don't understand
a lot of the Bible and your story. But I
do know you are love. And I'm so glad.
I know you are a third of my Higher
Power. God...Father, Son, Holy Spirit.
That part has always been easy for me to
accept. Don't know why. But I haven't
got *hung up* on that one. Thanks.

Jesus, when things get all *fussy*...
you know...when a lot of us humans
don't understand you in the same way...
I figure that's ok. Because we're all
different people with different views.
That's the way you made us. You know...
I believe when you walked out of your
grave...you didn't look left or right. You
just walked straight out into the world
to share yourself. Love for everyone.

Jesus, I know I fall short of being like you.
Kinda silly to even phrase it that way. I
mean there's no way I can be just like you.
But I know I sure ought to try harder. I'm
such a *slacker* much of the time. I'm
sorry. All I know to do is to ask for your
forgiveness and keep goin'. Of course
if I'd just shut up and let you run things...
this whole relationship thing would probably
be a lot smoother. *Fewer hitches.*
Lord, hang in here with me please. Thank you.

Jesus, I have an issue I want to talk about.
It's about all the other Gods people follow in
this world. I was taught You are The Way.
And I believe that. But I don't want people
going to the hell that I was taught about in
my younger years. I mean, here's the way
I feel. The first twenty years of my life I
was severely depressed. It was pure horror
and terror. If hell is that bad or worse...I
don't want anyone to have to endure that
for an eternity. I know there is a lot of evil
that has to be dealt with...but God...well,
I'm gonna trust you have it figured out for
everyone's good. I'll just concentrate on
sharing your love. I trust you.

Jesus, here I am at the age of 56 years.
A lot has happened in my life. Some good
some bad. You know my trials. You

have been with me all the way...even when
I couldn't feel you...you were holding me.
You gave me endurance. Thank You So Much.
I look forward to the years to come, here on
earth and in heaven. Even though sometimes
I have my doubts and think...what if you shut
the *Pearly Gates* and I'm left on the outside.
But I figure doubting is just normal for us
humans. That's all a part of the *faith thing*.

Jesus, thank you for all the people that are in
or have been in my life. You gave me such
great parents. Thank you! I've had some good
role models in all areas of my life. And most
of them were relying on You. That's nice...
how we can help each other out in this life.
Thank you for the material blessings you have
given me. So many are wanting. Have mercy
on them please. And help me to help them.
Thanks so much for so many friends! They
are wonderful to be around...even when we
have our *spats*. Goodness...will we ever
grow up! I can see you shaking your head.
Oh well. Thank you for being so patient.
Jesus, I guess I'll go to bed pretty soon. Keep
me safe tonight. And help me be at my best
tomorrow. Thank you for being you. Thank you
for loving me. Thanks for your easy access.
Help me to take more advantage of it. You are
not only The Way, The Truth and The Life...
You Are The Best...The Greatest!
Praise to You. I love You. Amen.

Nobody In The Neighborhood

I could say...*There goes the neighborhood.*
But no...Not that extreme for everyone.
Even so, that's what it feels like to me.
See...I've lost a neighbor. Not death. No.
Thank the Lord. Still, they are no longer
around. Missing from *their spot.*

The young, the old and all in between
hung out in the neighborhood. Fun times.
Not *fast times*. Rather a slow easy
Southern evening, closing days of whatever
you were made of. As for me...kinda lazy.
Lounging around. Sure. *I put in my time.*
Well...sorta. But those nights, so relaxing...
at least for me. I didn't have to put forth
much effort!

Now, gotta get used to what is not. It's
really not that big of a deal, considering
life in general. But damn. I miss my
neighbor. Fast, witty, fireball. Just a
few descriptions of the person. And an
atmosphere of carnival revolved around
the hours...all the shift. What needed to
get done...got done. Standards met...
sometimes above and beyond.

Well, crap. It's the way it is. Just life.
People come and go. Situations always
changing. Not necessarily all good or
all bad. But gotta get used to it. It feels
like there is nobody in the neighborhood.
Something to be said for the *personality*
of a person. We're all different. Thank
goodness. But I wish I had the personality
of my long gone neighbor to keep me
company.

Can't make just anybody be my neighbor.
Oh...they can *be there in person*. But what's
in that person? That's what counts. Friends
come along ever so often. You know...the
ones you want to *hear*. The ones that you
want to *listen*. To hear your insides and
shoot you a straight shot. But now...
Nobody is in the neighborhood.

Ok. Enough lamenting. Like said earlier...
just life. Make the most of it. I'll see that
past neighbor every now and then. So, it's
not like they've disappeared...to be forgotten.
Change. Ugh. Who really likes change?
Maybe after getting used to the change…
all is well. Maybe even better. But in the
meantime, *nobody is in the neighborhood*.

Solid

A wave crashes. Sand and silt swirl with
the current. Sinking? Swaying? Faltering?
No. Standing straight and tall. Upright...
prepared for all the elements of nature.
Walking on water? No Way! Just saying
a prayer every day...for the day.

The fire in the mind...ashes blown into the
wind. Gone...hoped for good. But not forgotten.
Never forget the past. Always a reference
for the present and future. A guide. Tried
and proven. No, don't forget what has been.
But don't live and relive a miserable existence.
Come to terms and let go. Accept peace.

Give of self graciously. So many at a loss.
Looking, striving, surviving. There is hope!
It can be. Bad can turn to good. Pain can
change to a comfortable ease. Purpose...
it can be found. This fortunate soul sings.
Once voice only screamed...or was too
stifled to speak. Now...melody and harmony
can be felt and heard by self and others.

What is the direction? Not sure...in a specific sense. But it is a positive course. Never did this life ever expect to truly live. Always death knocking on the door of a disassembled mind. Now...throw back the sashes! Open the windows! Let the calm, clear, refreshing breeze inside...give hopeful breath to others.

It's Solid. It's Thanksgiving in the Spring!

Rice and Refineries

Gumbo wasn't just somethin' you ate.
The black, sticky, thick, cement-like earth.
The Gulf Coastal Prairie of Southeast
Texas. Runnin' from Port Arthur to...
oh, I don't know...Freeport. In the northern
corner...The Big Thicket pines scattered
to an end. And all the while...flat.

Rice built our house, paid our bills and
fed us. Rice and gravy...most every Sunday.
I didn't know rice came in a box until I was
in high school. I never thought about it.
It was just always in a big brown burlap tow
sack in our pantry. Daddy brought it home
from his work. His occupation was to prevent
insect destruction to the crop.

We knew families and generations of families
that were rice farmers. Of course, throw in
the soybeans. And all the occupations that
surround agriculture. The massively tall tan
rice dryers. Amelia and Elizabeth...right next
to the railroad tracks, appropriately. I took my
turn working with rice quality in a laboratory.
It was a great part-time job during college.
And then a short stint full-time.

One of the prettiest sights... Acres and acres of
lush, green blades of the rice plant. So, so green.
Never mind 98 degrees and snakes. No, thinking
more like the late afternoon of an overcast day.
Sun breaking at its setting, to give light to the beauty.
Flat, flat earth that every once in awhile is interrupted
by a rice canal. That's where we set out trotlines.
And oh yeah...about using blackbirds for target
practice. Two-fold benefit. Yes...there is more to
rice than just a tiny little grain.

We were right where it started...Spindletop.
Black gold...so the song says. Mighty refineries
brought people from everywhere. I mean everywhere.
A lot of first generation Southeast Texans.
Most of my friends' fathers worked in the maze of
pipes, valves and laddered towers. Of course, there
were those *out in the field*. That smell. That air.
You just get used to it. And if you were born near it...
you didn't have to get used to it. It just was. Strange
how an otherwise bad odor can generate fond
memories.

The long hours. The different shifts. Graveyards.
Friends' fathers had legitimate reasons for not having
to be in church for every service! "We have to be
quiet. My dad is sleeping." The dangers abound.
One afternoon I watched out my parents' bedroom
window as Goodyear exploded into a huge torch.
Structures falling, we prayed safety for those we
knew and all involved. People from far off might be

too hasty if they judge the environment. We all know the benefits. It's what makes much of the world go round. There's always a price to be paid. Hopefully, scientists and engineers of the future will perfect the process. But it is what it is.

At 56 years of age, I live in the hills. Far from the coastal prairie. I have made my home. It is good. But when people ask where I'm from, I always start my reply with... "Well, I'm originally..." and I have to tell about the Rice and Refineries. Strange how so many of us just wanted to *get outta town* when we graduated from high school. Never did I imagine I'd be so proud to be a product of Rice and Refineries. And what really *made it*...were a lot of good people!

Stalled

The season's over. We lost the finals.
Exhausted from the hype.

The doctor's leaving. Not another lined up.
Certain amount of anxiety of future aid.

The apartment continues to not get clean.
I really don't give a shit.

We could consider weight loss, bad habits, etc.
But let's not.

The most is not made of the time on hand.
I'll think about it tomorrow.

The photo album project sits in the corner.
Oh...save it for a cold winter day.

Am I despondent? No. Am I sad? No.
Am I lonely? No. Am I discouraged? No.

Well? Well...I'M HOT!!!!!!!!!
I'M HOT!!!!!! It's consistent triple digit
heat index days and IT'S NOT EVEN JULY!!!!!

HELL!!!!!! HADES!!!!!!!! LORDY MERCY!!!!!
LIKE SHARING A ROOM WITH SHADRACH,
MESHACH AND ABEDNEGO!!!!!!!!!!!!!!!!!!
Or however their mother spelled their names.
Wait a minute. Things turned out alright for them.
Anyway...You get the drift. IT'S HOT!!!!!!!!!

Ok. So it's summer and I'm Stalled. Don't count
the days. Don't expect a cool breeze out of nowhere.
Don't think things will get accomplished without
effort. Just suck it up. Wipe my brow. And hold
on till football season!

From Beaumont To Salem

It began early morning. Excited the
night before. Miserably ingesting
crushed Dramamine in jelly, so as
to avoid the bitterness. This process
began half an hour before the ride.
What seemed a lifetime prior, brought
great respect to the *magic pill*...
which I still could not swallow.
The 60's we packed the little green
Valiant. By the 70's it was the big
green Fury III. Daddy's favorite color.
The *boat* of a car...the Fury...had
air condition AND a radio! Absolute
unnecessities that we could finally
afford.

By the time we got to Lumberton
community...we were in another country.
And we had just begun! We were on our
way to Arkansas. Daddy, me, Momma
in front. Mark and Cindy had not yet
started claiming territories of the back
seat...not yet. Stakes were sure to be made.

The pine trees gradually got thicker and
the ground sandy. With the air conditioner...
less smell of the Evadale paper mill. Slowly,
incline and decline made the lay of the land.
We were already gettin' closer to the hills.
Or so it seemed. We had 11 more hours to go.

As we neared Jasper, we knew we were on a vacation. Because of the lakes. Our friends... their summer destinations and family gatherings involved the lake country. But we had a long ways to go to get to blood. The nearest family was Ft. Worth. And that was only a trip or two. But one involved Six Flags Over Texas...trips I barely remember. Too young. Anyway... back to the eastern trek.

By San Augustine, if there had been no nausea... I was *out of the woods*. Even though we were definitely deep in the woods. Thinking about the noon meal. For a number of years a family restaurant in Marshall served us well. For the life of me, I can't remember the name of the eatery. If Momma was alive, she'd remember. Well...on second thought. Oh well. Good food. Oh yeah...think the Lions Club had their emblem hanging. Had to be good!

As for stops...there were not many. Early years meant an open car door for discretion...on the side of the road...and a roll of toilet paper. Green and white water cooler jug. Don't remember cups. Just drank out of the spout. You know...back then there just wasn't much between Beaumont and Texarkana. At least the stretches between populations were lengthy. In it for the long haul!

Nearing Texarkana, I prepared myself. I wanted
to be the first to cross over into Arkansas. Therefore
I slouched way down in the seat, and stretched my
leg to where the tip of my toe was the furthest in
the front floorboard. It worked! I was first! Ok.
The Red River was true to its name. Oh...lest
I forget the opportunity to use the bathroom at
the nice Arkansas tourist bureau. And we always
got another map. Momma was sure to strike up
a conversation with other travelers in the women's
restroom. Then we'd hear *their story* for the
next 10 miles. Ugh.

The first stop in Arkansas was Great Aunt Ava's.
She and Uncle Lewis lived in Prescott. Their
daughters were older than us. But all in all we
did get to see them quite often. In the *Valiant
Years*, we would spend the night with them.
Breaking the trip into two days. But with the
newfound luxury of the Fury III and better
highways, the travel was faster. Limiting the
drive to one day. Anyway...regardless...
The most important thing about Aunt Ava's...
she always had Coca Cola on hand! Since we
didn't keep them at home...this was A Very Big Deal!
And she bragged and made over us kids. "Aunt Brag"

Back on the road, we made our way towards
Little Rock. When we got to the city, we began
to look for the domed capitol building. Crossed
the Arkansas River...which still looked similar

to our Texas rivers. If we were making good time, we stopped to see Uncle John and Aunt Valda for a bit. Then hit the road again...continuing northeast. The land was basically flat, compared to what we would eventually enter into. It was Beebe, Searcy then Bald Knob. That's where it began. The climb.

Going due north the land became more and more hilly. Curves began. Yet *flat* was still part. Until. Until Batesville. Then it really began... *Our Arkansas*...the foothills of the Ozarks. The giant...I'm talkin' giant curve leading into Batesville made for some tense moments. After the descent off the curve, we crossed the White River. Greenish, clear, clean water. We loved to kid Momma...a one-time contestant of the White River Beauty Contest. She never really laughed about it. It was kinda like she had been *living on the edge* during that time. Hahaha. Whatever.

Population was sparse between towns. Continuing north we made it to Cave City. Home of the World's Sweetest Watermelons. So they claim. Indeed, they were and are delicious. So, now Mark and Cindy had to share the back floorboard with at least one...sometimes two watermelons Daddy had thumped and considered *just right*. By this time everyone was getting irritable. We were almost to our destination...yet about two hours away.

There had probably been arguments and non-violent fights. But the mood soon turned to semi-excitement. Relatives to be seen and plans of swimming and fishing began occupying our minds. We were goin' to a little county seat town that had a square around the courthouse. Dime stores and a drugstore that had a soda fountain. It was Salem, Arkansas. And the welcome was the Salem Knob...a good-sized hill... small mountain. We were gonna be let loose to run all over creation with no fear of harm. And cousins and cousins.

But we weren't there yet. We continued north through Evening Shade and then to Ash Flat. Turning west on Highway 62, we were on the homestretch. Another 16 miles of hills, curves and nothin'. Save two signs that signified the communities of Agnos and Glencoe. It would be between 8 and 9 o'clock at night. The lights were on bright most of the time...as there was hardly any traffic.

Finally, we round the last curve and hill. There...the Salem city limits sign. Always noting if there had been an increase in population since the last trip. If the moon was bright, we could distinguish the Knob. Soon taking a left on Highway 9 South...we pass the log Legion Hut. (That's where Momma had her bridal shower.) And then there it was...the little rock house. The Fury goes upward as we cross into the driveway. This sheds the spotlight on the Perryman home. Movement can be seen inside...and soon it pours outside. We made it! As I take my first step out of the car there is one drawback. I'm not barefoot. Too many rocks and no soft San Augustine grass. But let the Good Times begin!

Humbly, We Walk

They say a time for everything.
And so our stride. In the eve of
despair we crawl to a stop. Cries,
moans, heartaches evolving into
numbness. We can never be the
flagship of the person born to the
skin. Will we always falter? Always
less than? Will we disrespect ourselves
to a constant grovel? Wait. That is
not our lot.

On top of the world. We dance, run,
skip carefree about the nature of daily
living. We don't lie to ourselves. We
know the good life is not portioned out
every day. But we go with it. It's great!
A happiness abounds. Are we better than?
No. But it feels good to be the winner.
We're not *showing off*. But the ecstasy
can't be hidden. Maybe a bit too bold
at times. Will our confidence be blurred
to the grandiose? Let's not let it.

Too little or too much. There must be a
balance. Yes, there are the depths...
and also the heights. Our navigation
determines how we sit in the middle.
Boring? No. Stability? Yes. So, at

times we cannot pull ourselves out of the mire. Not long after, we may be donning the gold medal of the marathon. But for the main...we pace ourselves. And humbly, we walk.

The Most Important Man

The most important man I know is leaving. He's been the closest male relationship in my life. And a role model indeed. Giving and sharing love, care and support through my entire life. He is my Father. A great Dad. And I always have, and continue to call him *Daddy*.

He needs full support in clothing himself. And the wheeled chair is his rocker. He sits dozing off and on. Rarely is he *on target* with topics showing on the television screen. Sharing meaningful time watching the Razorbacks are most likely over. I don't know. We'll see.

Conversation with Daddy is very limited now. But he knows who I am. As well as my brother and sister on the phone. We've been blessed. His mood is pleasant. Another gift from God. And he seems comfortable and content. He has been blessed by his 91 years of life. And he has been a blessing to others for a lifetime.

He is at the door. Only God knows when
the threshold will be crossed. But what's
on the other side? Oh My Goodness!!!
There she'll be waiting...after the Heavenly
Father welcomes him in. He held her hand
till the end. And she'll reach out for his...
to a new beginning. There's no sadness.
It'll be pure joy. Oh yes, here on earth we
will mourn our loss...but the losing process
has already prepared our minds and hearts.

When the morning comes, he may have left.
Or...he may hang around for a good while yet.
Regardless, it is so wonderful that no
individual has to set the timetable. It's
definitely all in God's hands. He sleeps in a
bed that is less than a mile from where he
was born. A beginning...and right now just
a *Rest and Relax Station*. Sooner than
later, the door will swing open wide and
The Party Will Begin! (Make your reservations.)

Shades of Mourning

What to do with grief? Specifically,
grief due to the loss of a loved one.
Cry. Yeah. Laugh. Yeah.
Remember. Yeah. Regret. Hope
not too much. Live. Yes, we live with
grief. We own it. We work with it.
We feel it. And hopefully it dissipates
to hold fond memories.

In the hours before our life transforms
to the *life after another*...we can only
walk with surety that life is indeed good.
And that's not a small lot. In fact, it is a
grand existence. To know we've known
the person who goes ahead. Counting
blessings, and remembering so many
answers to prayers in the lives lived.

So here we sit. Well, we're going through
the motions at the very least. Heck...things
may be mighty good. But still we have to
wait. We think. We think about what it's
all about. And we get nowhere. Because
there's nowhere to go. We wait. But at
the same time we busy ourselves. In a way...
everything is kinda *on hold*. Can be
frustrating to our life plan. What's that?
God holds the clock? Yep. So we live
with that fact. And it's all part of the stages
that help us let go.

Let go?! I'm gonna have to give up a
priceless gem? Well, yeah. That's how
it works. Wait. Do I make the grieving
all about me? No. Others are feeling the
loss. Show care towards them. That's
right. Get out of myself. Oh...go through
what I've got to go through internally...
Then open my mind and heart to let others
into the newness of life without the loved.

Shades of mourning surround. But they do
not consume. Days and hours are not
known. We walk and talk...and run and shout.
We take note of the newborn. There is life
to live among the dying. In fact, we grant
what's probably the last request of the one
leaving...we love...we care...we say our prayers.
And then we end, with the word...Amen.

Homemade Ice Cream

Summertime. Neighborhood get-togethers. Church parties. Mosquitos. Wiffle-Ball games. Volleyball...if somebody had a net. Floodlights. Cans of **OFF**. Chunks of salty ice. Wet newspapers. Cranks...then electric. Vanilla, Chocolate, Strawberry, Peach (Momma's specialty...using Arkansas peaches.) Fresh cut grass. HUMIDITY! Sweaty kids. Sundown and after. Loud laughing. Young crying. Tag. Hide and Seek. June Bugs. Moths. Skinned knees. Parents warning. Somebody gets left out. Teens leave and go somewhere. Adults juggle conversation, hosting, and refereeing fights. Fish Stories. Recipes. Vacation details. Blackened, baresole feet. Doors constantly open and close. Lawn chairs...some rotten...but still usable. Cars parked on the lawn. 9:00 p.m. and starting to wind down. Suggestion of future gatherings. Mess to clean up. Tired. Probably happy. Homemade Ice Cream.
B.B.B. (Before Blue Bell)

Too Much Me

Even with this explanatory write...
I again bow down to my turncoat ego.
Maimed by ridiculous obsessive brain
waves. But...anyway... Ah...such is
the burden I bear. Give me a break!
On with the words.

In actuality, I am totally responsible for
putting the burden on myself. Why?
It's just the way I'm built. Ugh. Well...
enough. Yes. I'm all about me. Wait.
Let's dissect that a bit. I do care about
others and consider my fellowman. I
lend a helping hand. I am a good friend.
Tell me more...

Well, there is just Too Much Me in my
mind. And it's not a *complimentary*
portion. No. It dredges and delves.
When in fact, there is no reason for the
endless search. A search leading only to
fleeting false security. Which matures
into despair. Not good.

The deal is the way I *feel*. Everything's
about the way I feel. Not that I think I
should feel better than others. No. It's
not thinking that I'm more important. It's

just too much. Too much figuring. I think
about How I feel...Why I feel...What I'm gonna
feel...and on and on. And it gradually dips
to the negative. So, at the very least I ride
with small bag of bullshit thrown over my
shoulder. Well...that's refreshing!

But in the positive...that *small bag* used
to be the size of a dumpster. And it carried
the weight of such steel. So things have
improved...Indeed...ALOT!!!! Thankful.
But you know, I'm tired of draggin' this small
bag around...ready to get rid of all of it!
So...How? Well, this written acknowledgement
is the beginning. Hmmm. There are some
positive aspects to *digging and hashing out*.
Yep. With this writing of *Too Much Me...*
I'm actually letting go of some of me.
BE GONE! Enough.

Empty Canvas

To start over? Not really. Just continuing on with life. Another stage in view. So it is...stages of life. Some...flourishing. Some...catastrophic. But somehow we survive and there is a new beginning...again.

I have a gallery filled with pictures. But there's always room for another. I've used all of the color wheel. Some paintings are pleasing to the eye. And some bring pain to the heart. A reminder of what was. And too...an illustrated warning of what not to do. Yes, I am responsible for some of the hurt. As I am the artist of very good times. Just life.

So, right now I sit in front of another empty canvas. Great! What do I want to do? Where do I want to go? What do I want to say? And it's not all about me. The world, you, my neighbor, strangers... all can be characters alive in living color.

I have some talents to explore further. As I type...I do. Go with it. Make the most of what I have. And all along be grateful. Gratitude for what was, is and what will be. So much freedom now. Freedom from torment, chains, and a tortured mind-set. Ahh...that gratitude.

Again...here I sit in front of an empty canvas.
I can have the world. Am I joking? No.
See, I don't have to have the world...to have
the world. To me...*having the world* is knowing
security, happiness, contentment, peace and love.
That's just some of what I already experience.
And there can be more!

I don't know what I want to paint. But right
now I'm just dabbling in the colors and
considering. That's great...I can sit and
consider what I want for the next stage of
my life. Sure, there'll be absolutes of images
in the painting. Lows and highs...and all in
between. But the theme...my perspective,
has a lot to do with that. As for now...
I'm in a *good spot*. Think I'll start with
a faint purple. Yes, a color of ease. Nice.

Once Burning

The fire...once a blaze lighting up the night, showing the way. Such warmth and comfort. Paths were cleared, and the brush could be used appropriately for keeping the fire at a steady burn.

The flame, always a necessary source in preparing essential nutrition. How we starve now. *Fan the flames...please keep the fire going!* Let us sit at a long table with plenty of entrees and side dishes. Fill us up. So hungry for solid food and comradery.

About the warmth... It's so cold now. And it's getting colder. We Need Heat! So hard to sleep when the temperature dips this low. And there's much to say with regard to the body heat of others. So far away. So distant. And the wedge continues to sever.

What's happened to the sun? Our ball of fire. Are we to only exist among shadows? How do we find our way? It's too dark. The moon sheds only so much light. Yes, the only time is nighttime. Will our days ever come back around? Has the earth come to a complete stop? God have mercy.

The fire...once a beacon for all.
Will it be reduced to embers...to
finally extinguish? God in heaven...
Have mercy on us. God...please.

Our Own Beach

Let's go to the beach! We're goin' to the beach!
White sand? Well...
Clear, blue/green water? Well...
Spotlessly clean environment? Well...
Big umbrellas with attractive beach furniture? Well...
Ice cream and snack vendors? Well...
Good lookin' lifeguards? Well...
Huge waves for the surfers? Well...
Expensive condos? Well...

Well...hell...you said you were goin' to the beach?
We are! Our own beach! All ours.
Cross a swing bridge. High Island, Gilchrist, Crystal.
Light brown sand and brown/greenish water.
A lot of our beach color is due to the emptying
sediments of so many close rivers. Just natural.
No. Not for a postcard. Could be cleaner.

Bring our lawn chairs, towels, old blankets...
rig up tarps sometimes. Ice chests seats two.
Eat what we bring, out of the back of our cars and
trucks. Yes, we drive right out to the water...sometimes
in it. Damn. Don't get stuck! Yeah...we can find enough
sea shells to make us happy. At least we could.
Early years...plenty of sand dollars. Later...more tar.

Safety? Fend for yourself. Better know how to
swim with the tide. Get stung by a jellyfish or
man-of-war? Suck it up! Oh...if it hurts so bad
you throw up...might have to take some measure
of first aid. If lucky enough to have friends
with one of the weathered cabins...go recuperate.
What about sharks? Don't know. Just don't
think about it. So far...so good.

Recreation devices/gear? Hell...we're here.
That's enough. Well yeah...good for inner tubes.
Somebody brought a tractor inner tube? Awww Right!
Be careful about sunburns. Funny, the same sun
in Florida, California, Hawaii and Southeast Texas.
A burn is a burn! Pain is pain. So don't forget the
lotion. If overcast...hey maybe a storm brewin'...
surfers might get a taste of their heaven. Can only hope.

We have the seaweed, seagulls, crabs and other
creatures of nature. And a bit too much *unnatural
attractions...or eyesores*. Oh well...such as it is.
See...it doesn't matter...Cause it's ours! It's our sand.
It's our water. It's our rules. Rules which might be
considered broken. Well...we're gonna live forever!
And we don't have to drive far to get to our beach.
So, we can go at the *drop of a hat*. At least after
the age of 16...driver's license. Yep...on our own.
Honestly, we're lucky if we get to borrow our folks
car. So, probably don't get to go as much as we want.
And we get over it.
Let's go to the beach! We're goin' to the beach!
Our Very Own Beach!!!

Little Bird

It hurts to watch. It hurts to see.
It's a little bird. He can't fly very
well anymore. Actually, he can't
get off the ground. His wings are
tired and worn. Like the life of
most every bird...once he soared.
No longer.

It hurts to watch. It hurts to see.
The little bird no longer has a
nest. Oh...he makes do. The best
to be expected. Out of the elements.
But...not the same. The little bird
has had a good life. But all life
ends. At least, breath on this earth.
What's that? "I'll fly away."
Yes. There is promise and future.

It hurts to watch. It hurts to see.
The little bird can't help himself
too much anymore. He flutters
about at times. But really goes
nowhere. The little bird is lame.
It's hard to watch a lame little bird.
And it's hard to leave him alone,
amongst other lame birds every night.
It hurts to watch. It hurts to see.

Dirty Hair

Let's see. How to describe to those who are not warped? Hmmm. Talkin' about what is basically neurosis. You know... I never really understood that word until reading the dictionary definition. So basically...everything is of the negative. Looking inward...I realized...my whole thought processing had a negative base and surge.

Well, that's crappy. Yep. BUT in knowledge comes the ability to change! Things in and about me could be positive. But that positive vibe was flowing into a negative core. Ooh. Sounds bad. Well...it wasn't devastating. But all in all...when things would come full circle...thoughts or behaviors...there would be a good chance that a feeling of doom would settle, and claim a period of distress. Eventually, it would ease and drift away. But all of it was unnecessary. Huh!

Yes. It was all a false perception. Actually, it wasn't really how I perceived something... it was more a full force of emotional dread that came from...nowhere? Well. Why did it happen? I have no idea. I'm leaving the *figuring* to the belief that my mind can definitely *play tricks on me*. Oh...to leave the dissection so simplistic? YES! I'm not spending the rest of my life trying to make sense of the workings of my mind. Not with this issue. Just enjoying the release.

Ok. An example. Everything is going good. There are no problems that cause grief or stress. Confusion and depression are not to be found. All is well. So, I'm sitting playing solitaire on the iPad at the truck stop. Back up...I have not washed my hair in several days. Ugh. So, I have dirty hair. I need to wash my hair. I don't want to wash my hair. It seems such an effort. There is some guilt for not doing this simple but necessary task.

Back at the truck stop... I'm playing on the computer...evidently...maybe the thought that I need to wash my hair glides through my thought processes. It grabs ahold of any emotions that just happen to be hangin' around in my body. And it immediately evolves into an intense wave of semi-fear. Shifting and settling to dread and doom. And there's some nausea. A burden to bear. For a period of time, everything about my being is negative. Yes. There's no way out. Not fun. And all because I haven't washed my hair?! Well. Hell...I don't really know.

Honestly, it probably is not the fact and thought. It just happens to be the straggling emotion that has nothing better to do than make me feel shitty.

Are you still with me? Ok. So, one night... at the truck stop...playing cards...I visualized how this was happening. WOW! An enlightenment! Yes. And what was I able to do? Well...in a few minutes after I realized what neurosis or whatever it was, did to me...I thought... I Don't Have To Feel This Way! I Have A Choice. I Don't Have To Feel Bad! There is really nothing to feel negative about! WHOA!!!! YAY!!!!!!!!!!! FREEDOM!!!!!! That was about four months ago. Do you have any idea how happy my life is now?!! Prayers continue to be answered! GOD IS GREAT!!!! GRATEFUL.

(This is a *next day edit*. The thing I was able to do...I was able to say, my dirty hair has nothing to do with this bad feeling. In fact, the bad feeling in and of itself has no merit. Therefore I have a choice. I do not have to feel this eerie aura. It is baseless. I separated the dirty hair and put it in one category. That left me with a category that held the bad feeling. And there was no reason to have a *bad feeling category!* Wah Lah!!)

Floatin' In Space

It took years of preparation...ever since birth...to come to this point. To float freely in space. Only a thread of attachment. Someday that will be gone. And probably not too far in the future. For all practical purposes, I've been floating along very well for quite some time now. Save...just a strand.

It is not necessarily scary. Maybe some apprehension at times. But I've been taught so well...how to spacewalk.
My spacesuit is functioning properly, and has a reliable source of energy...from above. Or...really since I'm already in space...which way is heaven? Hmmm. So, His Spirit existing in my spirit is the key to infinite strength and power.

Lost In Space...remember the television show? No...I'm not lost and looking for direction. Even though I'm not 100% sure I'm on track all the time. No...I'm not. But that's ok. That's the reason for faith. "Faith of Our Fathers"...how well they made sure that was supplied. Oh, I had to accept and develop. But they were my guide. So grateful.

I don't feel much gravity right now.
What to expect? I'm floatin' in space.
Things are light. There is not dread or
heaviness of thought and emotion. I've
been in training for this moment for
a lifetime. Most people have other vital
connections besides their "parental units."
(Coneheads! Thanks SNL) For me, I
really don't. Not taking lightly other family
members or friends. Wait...I'm not one of
a kind. There are others like me.

Right now there is a bit of a hollowness.
I guess some things can never be replaced.
But the future looks bright. Again...not
totally set on my agenda. But it's alright.
Because...I'm alright. Yes. "It Is Well
With My Soul" So many prayers have
been answered in the years of preparation.
Once floundering in misery and fear.
Now...floatin' freely in space. And I'll
bet I become more comfortable, and in
tune with this vast space as time passes.

The future. Yes. I see *fun* when I look
into my crystal ball. Ahh...a positive tone.
Such an acquisition! Times past...everything
negative and lifeless...save the beating pulse
of self-degradation. So glad I'm not there
anymore. Thankful. So, I'll continue to
let myself float in space with ease. Not

complicate nature. I believe the unsettled vagueness of the present state...will eventually solidify to a sure sense. And I'll not only be floatin' in space...well...I just might be dancin' in space! Turn up the music!

My Sister And I

My sister and I...we disagree.
She's right. I'm wrong.
I'm right. She's wrong.
Whatever. So be it. We
disagree. Are the stakes high?
Only if we let the world dictate
our relationship.

My sister and I...we share.
The same father. The same
mother. The same brother.
We share the same love we
were taught and given. Such
stability was ours. Our parents'
care cultivated our futures.
And here we are...we love each
other.

My sister and I...we prepare.
We look forward to a time when
stresses and divisions will no longer
be. Here on earth? Probably not.
But what did we learn in our youth?
A faith. A faith that has a future.
We both claim that faith...it's ours.

My sister and I...
Let us disagree. Let us share.
Let us prepare. Let us use the love
that faith allows, to protect the very
core that binds us together. Someday...
one day...we will sit side by side in
Heaven's sunlight, sharing an
unfathomable love and singing...
"Love Divine, All Loves Excelling"

I Want To Care

I want to care. I want to share.
I don't want to run and hide.
I don't want to be shamed or
cause others to feel *less than*.
Sometimes it's so hard to care.
Not lacking the ability. But taking
the chance to let ourselves be let down.

Do we have to be right? Are we doomed
to be wrong? That is...if we take a chance
and care. True enough...we are going to
experience success and defeat. Such is
life...the good and the bad. Really?
Such a lightweight, simplistic attitude
and view? Don't you have any depth?
Oh...if you only had a glimpse of the
bottom of this well! It goes on and on!
Unfortunate for the psyche.

So to step back from the brawl...perhaps
on occasion. Even if there is great
importance to the matter. Strange...
Sometimes we have to *not give a flip*...
to protect our ability to give the utmost
care. Oh...to be so whimsical. Living
in a dream world? Well...it's more like
survival. Surviving so as to show
care once more.

It can be so unpleasant to care. Feelings involved. Everybody's feelings involved. Ugh. The best and the worst. We have to take it all. If we do indeed care. But we can be careful when we care. Don't allow ourselves to be blindsided. Don't be a doormat. Consider pros and cons. Think before we speak. Oh man...whoa!

So, what of all this write? What's the point? Well...sometimes when we care, it makes us want to cry. And sometimes we feel like crying, because we feel like nobody cares. But we can't let tears take away our caring. No! We must hold on strong...and hold out our hand for our fellowman. Right, wrong, good, bad...regardless...Continue to Care. Continue to Share. Blessings are bound.

Lightning Strikes

Lightning strikes...it spreads a spark.
Lightning strikes...it breaks a heart.
The thunder rolls and windows rattle.
Two minds that meet...a constant battle.

The nature of humans...so strained to like.
Conflicts, bouts sorely scar the night.
Retreat for respect to the opposing view.
Complete regard for the future due.

It happens to course through blood-filled veins.
This unpleasing sense that can cause a drain.
So give of self to each soul that's met...
The best side of one's life, to be seen just yet.

Blood Red Moon

Midnight drive taken with leisure.
Sky darker than usual. Air...cool for a
summer evening. It's a slow go for
16 miles east. Hills and curves not
too extreme. Traffic is light...as always.

Cheap Trick peaks at high decibels.
Sipping favorite fountain drink.
Vehicle vibration slowly eases
the stress, brought on by a very
unkind day. Relax and let the wheels
roll down the well-worn path.

Destination? Does it really matter?
Like most times...looking for an
unexpected gem in the 5 dollar cd
bin at Walmart. Everything casual
and calm. So deserved.

Return trip just as serene. No
purchase made. Not necessary
for fulfillment. *Poor girl's getaway*.
This particular night...by the cast of
a blood red moon.

Evaporating

There it goes. More of me.
Well...more of what my mind
has been. Oh no! I'm losing
my mind. Hmmm. I guess...
in a way...YES!!!!!

Should I be scared? It seems
something so bizarre would
cause an anxious state. THAT'S
what I'm getting rid of! All the
thinking that causes that anxiety.

So YAY!!! I'm Losing My Mind!
The mind that for a lifetime has
brought misery, fear and pain.
Does this mean I don't have thoughts
and ideas? No. Not at all. They're
still there. It's just that they are not
surrounded and accompanied by all
the chaotic mind-crap. Or whatever.

I think what I'm trying to say...
I'm letting go of the feelings associated
with every thought that goes through
my head. Awww Right! Am I gonna
miss good feelings? No. Because the
immediate thoughts with regard to my
every move...were usually negative.

I'll still feel happy and glad. And I'll
still feel sad and bad. So...so, I'm still
gonna get unnerved and shaky at times?
Yes. But the *every split-second thought*
I hold in my mind, is no longer driven
by dissenting perspective of self.

So, here I sit tonight. More of me
continues to evaporate. And what's on
the horizon? FUN! Good Days!
Relaxation! Peace! Yes...more peace.
Answers to prayers that I've never prayed.
Because...I had no exact concept of the
depth of my mind-trap. Gratitude Indeed!
God Is Good!

Bowling Hill Nights

Goin' to the old homeplace.
In other words...going to my
Dad's childhood home. Actually,
he was the product of a wooden
house of The Depression. Later,
the 1940's big rock house took its
place. But on the same hill.
The Bowling Hill.

By the time I came on the scene,
the hill had been cut in two. A
highway was carved into the family
property. So, the status of being a
hill was more pronounced. The highway
department made concrete steps from
the bottom of the hill...the road...to the
top of the hill...now the front yard.
A great view off the front porch.
All just barely inside the city limits of
a small town in north central Arkansas.

Thirteen children were raised on the hill.
My Dad being the 6th in line. Eight boys.
Five girls. From the same two parents.
Family gatherings occurred in the summer
and winter. And things could get busy and
crowded! Cousins, cousins, cousins.
And the food...oh yeah! But eating was
secondary to us youngsters. It was all
about playing. And there were all ages.

Summer nights on the hill. Wow! You
would think that with a full day of relatives,
we'd be tired by sundown. Not so. Way atop
of the hill we had a front row seat to anything
happening...as far as comin' and goin' of traffic.
Waiting for the ferry traffic from Lake Norfork
was a continuous event. The lake was about
30 miles west. The ferry crossing the lake
could hold probably 18 cars. We could *time*
when the ferry *let out*. Growing up, this
was the totality of the night traffic...along with
18 wheelers. Of course, during daylight hours
we did our best to get the trucks to blow their
horns. Raising and lowering our arms and fists.

Lightnin' bugs...or some call them Fireflies...
Caught as many as we could to light up a jar.
Revolving games of chase, tag and hide-n-seek.
Oh...we had toys...water guns especially come
to mind. But it seemed most of our play was
interactions of *pretend-like* and such as that.
Some fights and pouting. But no murders that
I know of. That I know of...

One game that we drummed up...I loved.
It was called *Funny Farm*. Here's the deal.
We stand on the concrete walk in the front yard.
As soon as we see the headlights of an oncoming car...
we had to run in a circular pattern and touch each
designated base. The bases were a bush. A tree
that everybody climbed during the day. Also, you

had to touch a side of the house. Finally, end up back at the walkway. If you didn't make it back by the time the car reached the bottom of the hill...
You had to go to The Funny Farm. Which was the other side...the dark side...the scary side... of the cellar. And you had to stay till somebody took your place. In my mind, it was just assumed that The Funny Farm was for crazy people. In other words...an insane asylum. In fact, I believe that was the consensus among all of us. It's just that some of us did end up in a Funny Farm of sorts, in adult years! Hahaha. Oh well...

So, tired and worn out...and hot and sweaty... it was time to go in for the night. That meant taking a bath in *that* bathtub. Now...the tub was modern enough. But there was a window not too far above it. It was covered for discretion. But I was always afraid of spiders and bugs that lingered around the splintered window wood. And I had to stay in there till I was at least halfway clean and no more ticks. Yuck. But once beside my sister in the rollaway bed, my Dad pulled the cord to the light bulb. I went to sleep with a cool breeze blowing through the screens. And the sound of crickets and Whippoorwills.

Winter nights on the Bowling Hill were not as easy. I say that with respect to the temperature. A lot of times outside, there was snow on the ground. And a couple snowmen in the front yard!

But there was always the warmth of a Christmas tree. The only *official* heat in the uninsulated house... was a small pot-bellied wood stove. It was in the front room or the living room. It could also warm the dining room. Then add the heat from the kitchen...these areas were where we stayed until bedtime. With a big, big family...things could be very, very crowded! After Christmas Day...there would be added toys. Some of my cousins seemed to get Mr. Potato Head every year. There were always ears, hands and noses scattered about. Always careful not to step on and break cousins' gifts. Harder than you might think.

There was all the holiday foods and candies. Grandpa always gave each of the grandkids a Book of Lifesavers. Everybody loved that. Grandpa was also crazy about puzzles and games. The kind that you *figure out*. He had a handbag full of the tangible mindbenders. By the time I came along, my Grandmother had already passed away...so we had Grandpa's full attention. If you looked under Grandpa's pillow...you would find...a flashlight, Horehound candy, Lifesavers, Absorbine Jr. and maybe a Farmer's Almanac. I do believe when he was actually in bed...his teeth were also under his pillow. (I know this because he lived a couple of months with us, during the winter time. And I was a nosy little brat.)

Well, when it was time to go to bed during the winter...ugh. Except for the rooms mentioned earlier, the rest of the house was COLD!!!!! But the bathroom did have one of those little gas heaters with bricks. But it was too dangerous to leave on during the night. So, you just better not need to go! Layers and layers of night garb. Blankets and more blankets. Then came electric blankets! At last, some real comfort for my scrawny butt that had been spoiled by central air and heat! Hahaha But when you woke up in the morning...*you had to face it*. I distinctly remember early one morning I HAD to go to the bathroom. I was sleeping with my sister as usual. She made radical threats to me...if I were to disturb the warmth. In a brash flash, I flung all the covers off both of us and ran to the bathroom. All the while I could hear her hollerin' at me. Hahaha. And all this before storm windows and doors.

To the present. The Bowling Hill is still in our family. We continue to meet...those of us who can... on Memorial Day Weekend and a short time in the fall. I have not slept a night on the hill since my teenage years. But I am so very, very fortunate to have such fond memories of many childhood nights. Nights in a house, where a great number of some very fine and loving people have laid their heads. That being...
The family of Tollie and Ethel Bowling.

More, More!!!

The other night I was sitting playing solitaire.
A feeling semi-surfaced. No! Really??
Well...on with it. I wasn't sure what I'd felt.
It wasn't negative. But it wasn't sky high
positive either. I let my mind just be. And
soon the word *confident* came to the forefront.

Now, I've never considered myself a very
confident person. But what's this? Is
something developing? I'd just always
assumed the meaning of confidence was
believing you could do something. Then I
thought...perhaps there's more to being confident
than my lifelong...perhaps limited understanding.
Well...get out the dictionary. Yes. I still use
the actual book. I like tangible. Anyway...

When I looked up the word confidence, it
stated among other things...having belief in the
reliability of a person or thing. Hmmm.
That was a bit different. Reliability. I believe
I'm a reliable person. I always have. Hmmm.
Something to let *sink in* and settle. Tinge of
positive lurking. Oh No! Haha

Then reading more...it stated taking confidence a bit further...you have assurance. Ok. Surety. That sounds reasonable. But then I read part of the definition of assurance. It said...*shown as undisturbed calm*. BINGO!!!!!! Wow!! I Like That. Undisturbed Calm! Do you have any idea how appealing those words are to an individual with mental issues? **It's Heaven! Absolutely.**

So, I'm just letting the meaning of confidence become more familiar...by not obsessing about it! Yes. I'm just letting it evolve. There has not been any other grand enlightenment since. But...Lord... that's enough to do me for awhile. Think I'll just see which direction this takes me. I do know... It's All for the Positive!!!! Thanks God.

Own It!

It's a feeling. Kinda uncomfortable.
Like a stream of fear, doubt, disbelief
is edging around the perimeter of my
being. SO WHAT?!!! What's New?

That's it. It's a feeling. There is no
substance to present a meaning or
cause to its existence. It just is.
It's part of my body's circulation at
this moment. That's all!

The feeling is part of me right now.
Just at this minute. May be gone the
next second. Doesn't matter. Don't
run. Don't hide. Don't jump to conclusions.
Just own it. And be done with it. The End.

Brief Thoughts for the "Feel-Good"

A bit frivolous. Not skittish.
An air of freshness. Not stagnant.
Hear the tune. Disregard the lyrics for now.
Step with lightness. Don't pause in regret.
Live for the moment. Don't look at the clock.
Know you're true. Don't fear the lie.
Breathe slowly. But don't hold your breath.
Imagine kindly. Dispel anger.
Claim what's yours. Don't cling to belongings.
Smile inside. Smile outside.
Nurture wholeness. Let self, evolve with ease.
Get familiar with faith. See the frailty of doubt.
Sleep well this night. And share tomorrow.

Seein' After

What do you do? I see after.
What? No. I mean...what is your
occupation? I'm a see-afterer.
Come again? Ok. Right now in
my life I *see after* my Dad.

Oh...so you're a caregiver? No.
You're a caretaker? Not really.
I'm a see-afterer. My Dad is in the
nursing home...so he has assistance
with his daily life needs. I don't
have to do a lot to be a see-afterer.
Not physically. But mentally is a
different story.

Tell me...what does a see-afterer do?
What are the necessary job skills? Well...
as far as my situation goes...my number
one task is to go and visit my Dad. Let
him know he is not alone. Make sure he
realizes that our family unit still exist.
Regardless of deaths and distances.

What are some other tasks? Hmmm...
Keep the nursing home scene *up to snuff*.
Show up at different hours to check on
him. They never know when I might appear.
It is easy. I live close to the facility. And

I enjoy going and seeing him. I like most
of the staff and they do their job well. Oh...
they know I'll let them know if I'm not pleased.
This is a very Big part of being a see-afterer.
Maybe the most important skill. And I'm
damn good at it!!!

As a see-afterer, I also make sure my Dad
gets to talk to my brother and sister by phone
every week. I keep him *in the loop* of what
I know of their lives. Hound nieces and nephews
for recent pictures of their children. That would
be my Dad's great grandchildren. He has plenty
of photos of family on his walls and on his
night stand. Since my Mother passed away...
the big family portrait now hangs in his room.
Used to be in hers. It really is a good photograph.
A high school friend that is a photographer did
the work. A great job! Dated 2002.

My Dad's mail comes to my mailing address.
So, I'm into all his paper work...well, to a degree.
Thankfully, my cousin that lives here in town
is good with bookkeeping. I am Not a *numbers
person* at all! So...she takes the brunt of that job.
I do the literal footwork, with regard to the books.
But it's her mind that adds and subtracts and
organizes it all on her computer. She's a saint!
Avoiding what would be a disaster if it was
left up to me. Truly grateful.

I make sure Daddy has necessary clothing and such. You learn fast when enough, is enough of *stuff,* in a nursing home room. So, I gradually discard of what has become crap. That would usually be things that he still sees a need for...but it is junk. You know...like a cheap flashlight that doesn't work...that has sticky stuff on it...not sure if it's food, medicine, or...well, let's not go there. Ugh. Usually, this job takes great discretion. You have to be sneaky at times!

My Dad still owns a home here in town. I check on it. Make sure repairs are done. Let the water drip during cold, cold weather. Have it ready for my brother and sister for when they come to visit. We've done a lot of culling and downsizing of material possessions...so things are in order. The house still holds a few keepsakes that will one day be handed-down. His house is right down the road from my home...so everything's easy. Well...that might be an overstatement...sometimes. Anyway.

As far as legality goes...I'm his power of attorney. So, I'm involved in all decisions pertaining to his welfare. I do not feel burdened by this. I know what he wants. And if he doesn't know what he wants...I have a good idea what it would be. It's called being a daughter. Or at least it is part of my definition as his daughter. We all have our roles in life. Everybody varies and has a place.

I'm fortunate that I've been given the opportunity to be such a vital part of my Dad's last years here on earth.

Well, those are some tasks of a see-afterer. At least, those are the main points that come to mind... right off the bat. Sometimes it seems like I don't have to do much. Then other times it feels like I've got my plate full. So it goes. One thing... it can be very draining on the psyche if you don't *step back* from the situation every now and then. As far as my situation as my Dad's see-afterer...I continue to feel more and more blessed every day. Yes...I'm one lucky daughter. A blessed, fortunate and lucky See-Afterer. Just seein' after my Dad!

Limbo

The door can't be shut just yet.
The chapter is not finished. The
author has not penned the last word.
It can't be rushed. Don't want it
to be...but it is part of life. The
end of life. So it's all about learning
to live in the waiting.

Do I sound like a money hungry,
would be recipient of a grand will?
No. That's not me. Besides, the
material is not of a large scale.
So much more was given emotionally,
spiritually, physically while the main
of life was being lived. Absolute gratitude.

So what of it? I want the loved one's life
to take its natural course. And God will
see fit that it does. It's all in His hands.
Thank goodness. But it's this *spot* that
I find myself in...at this stage. Can't
quite step to the next phase of life. Have
to wait for timing of which I have no
control.

Living amongst dying. I guess that's what I'm striving to do. And the rest of my surrounding is rather limited. I mean, there is no *next generation* from me. Not that I feel cheated. I had no desire to be a parent. And I'm not overlooking nieces, nephews and their families. But they are at a distance. No. This is how l expected my life *to go*.

It's just...well, it's just what I said. I have to somehow learn to live forward, while waiting for an end to come. Right now, the situation has *played a game* with any structure I had involving a clock. Not that I've ever been an individual on a strict schedule. No. Everything has always been of a haphazard nature regarding my *game plan*. Given that...one might think I'd have better coping skills. Hold on. I'm coping well enough. But some things are just not easy.

I guess that sums it up. There are times in ours and everyone's lives that are not easy. We are not alone. In fact, one can be drawn closer to their Maker during this period. And also, a person can become more familiar with what's inside them...and what they're made of. So, that's much consolation. In fact, it could be considered a gift. Yes, I can say I know much more about myself than I did a couple of years ago. And it's good! Huh. How about that? Hmmm.

You know what I'm thinking? Just now as I have expressed myself in a cathartic nature... I've found a priceless aspect of this whole *waiting to die* stuff. Yes, I'm getting to know myself so much better. And there is a faith being honed. A faith in God, and a faith in myself. Someday it will be my turn...while others wait. And what better example to follow than my father. God Is Good.

The Element of Fear

The element of fear. What's it all about?
Not ghosts, goblins, murderers or life-
threatening situations. Not fear of the
unknown. Not fear of relationships.
Not fear for others. Not, not, not...
What the hell am I talkin' about?
What fear?

Well, the fear is within. Oh here we go!
God help us! We have to listen to psycho
garbage. No, no. It's nothing for which
we would have to go to the *nut hut*.
Well...that's a relief. I'm about tired of
that psychiatric shit. Now, now. Settle
down.

It has to do with the concept of *dis ease*.
Not feeling totally comfortable goin' about
our everyday life. Things are relatively
smooth. Everything is in place. Situations handled.
All is good. But that unpleasant vibe that flows
through our body and brain. Really...it's probably
all about *senses*. Oh...I don't know. I just
don't like it. Are you anywhere on the page of
which I'm talking? You're lucky if you're not.

So, anyway...I don't feel comfortable all the time.
Well...duh! Of course not. Not supposed to.
What do you expect? Heaven on earth? Well...
Ok...hold on. This is it. It's a *pestering* fear.
I'm pretty certain there is no substance to its
cause. So, there is truly nothing to be afraid of.
Again...back to the *senses*. Oh how well I
play that game. Me...the person who can feel
a leaf move. Yep. That's me. For better or worse.

Just waiting to feel apprehension. Is that it? Just sit
around ready to take my prescription of fear?
Senseless. That's it! Senses that are *senseless*.
Oh the humor. Well, some fear is appropriate. Yes.
If not, we'd soon be knocking on death's door.
Again... it is to our benefit to be afraid at times. But
this other crap. These other times that we are just
minding our own business...and a wave of
semi-doom sweeps. Ugh. But then we kinda
begin to expect those times for *it* to sweep.
Well. That sounds like a *set up* job on self!

Yeah. It's all in the goofy mind. So, what to
do? Just settle? Be bound to this uncalled for
frightful nuisance? NO. I'm not gonna live
a life that is less than. But I'm also not gonna
dissect and try to figure out what causes it.
That leads to the OCD Road! Yikes!! Nope.
Ok. I'm gonna do just what I'm doing right
now. I'm gonna write it to death! Haha

That's a good one. So, if you're still reading… you've witnessed the first exorcism of a *senseless sense*. And wouldn't it be cool if this is the last! Let's Hope!! Thanks for listening.

Shoestrings

Loose ends. That's what it kinda
feels like. Everything is at loose
ends. But not quite. Beginnings
and ends. Starts and finishes.
Life and death.

My loose ends are like good, clean,
sturdy shoestrings. The plastic that
keeps the ends from being frayed is
in topnotch condition. So, things are
lookin' good for the future. Believe so.

But the strings aren't tied. Hangin'
down and hitting the floor...but I'm
not tripping on them. No. I have
very good balance. I've been granted
a good portion of stability. Actually,
I've earned a lot of it. Experiences.
Yep. Learning experiences.

You know, taking the allegory further...
I don't feel as if my shoestrings are
being swept along the floor. It's more
like I'm sitting on a stool...feet dangling
down...and the strings are just hanging
in the air. And I feel comfortable as I
sit. In fact, I'm in a pretty good mood.
But my shoes are untied.

Well, so I have untied shoes. Again...
the strings are clean and sturdy. Walking
once more...I know my step will be stable.
I guess it comes to this...
At the right time, I'll get down off the stool.
Securely tie my shoestrings.
And walk with sure stride. Maybe some
hop, skip and jump added!

Stepped Out For A Spell

I feel like I checked out of life for
the past two or three days. Died?!!
No. I'm here as you live and read.
But I'm kinda drawin' a blank as to
what's been happening lately.

You see, I was coasting along...
dealing with everyday affairs and
responsibilities concerning my Dad.
When out of nowhere...Wait, honestly?
Out of nowhere? Try...out of my mind.
Ok. So, out of my mind appeared...
fear, anxiety and guilt. Oh...that's
pleasant. Yeah...really.

So, just because I was rattled I can't
account for my whereabouts? Well...
I know I didn't leave town. And I
slept at my apartment. I hung out
some at the truck stop. Wait. No,
I don't really think I spent much time
playing iPad card games. Hmmm.

Let's think back to the last thing I
remember. Ok. I was falling into
a paralyzing fear that I might be
inching toward a mild manic. Ok.
So I waded through severe apprehension
and ended it with a long period of sleep.

I do recall contacting my doctor. I probably wouldn't have given it much thought at this point...except she called me back, several hours ago. When things had kinda returned to normal. Normal? Haha. Well, anyhoo...

So...Whatcha been up to?

Wandering...Wondering

I no longer wander. And that's good.
I know where I belong. The town,
the state, the country...it's all in place.
And I'm sure of my abode. I like it.
An apartment that gives me all the
shelter and living area that I want
and need. I'm happy where I live.
I feel that my *house is a home.*
A sure comfort zone. Safety and
peacefulness exist. I'm a fortunate
soul...to no longer wander.

I no longer wonder...about everything.
Yes, I still wonder in the casual sense.
But no more constant questioning of
what was, what is, what will be. I
know who I am. I know what I like.
I know what my life's about. I know
what I believe about most things.
There are always going to be issues
not totally resolved. And I am resolved
of that fact. Ahh. That's nice. I know
my connections in life. That would be
the people whose lives interact with
mine on a daily basis. And they make
me feel good. I think I make them feel
good too. I'm a fortunate soul...to no
longer wonder...about everything.

Someday wandering and wondering
will totally be dispelled. Certainty will
be mine and yours. It begins with a
belief...here on earth. And that belief
springs the door open to heaven. But
for everyone...every being...
We must first take our turn in this world...
Wandering and Wondering.
Peace to you this day.

When There's Nothing To Hold Onto

It's easier to let go, when there's
nothing to hold onto. For over
half a century, clenching them
tightly in my fists. Fearful that
they be stolen by a short lifespan.

Not to be. She had 87 years. Such
a joy...even at the end, in her
disassembled mind. I say *a joy*.
But I really like to use the word
delight. Such a delight...my mother.
Even though she had some suffering,
in all actuality peace came soon and easy.
God's perfect timetable. And I let her go.
And for me...my experience...it was
easier to let her go...when most all of her
was already gone. I hear her sing in glory.
Even now...memories...such a delight.
And the future...will be once more.

He's 91 years old. My father still lives.
But it is becoming more and more the process
of simply breathing. He has not pained in
tremendous fashion. We've been so blessed.
But his frailty is gaining ground. His eyes dull.
His mind more confused. No longer to walk
or stand. Slowly drifting...drifting away from
me. He has been such a strong force...making

me the person I am today. Immense gratitude. But each day gets a little easier to open my hand wide...for God to reach down and take him home. And the future...will be once more.

Doe...A Deer

The deer...so innocent. The deer
in the headlights...could be naïve
or caught in the action. Doe, a female
deer...even more fragile and delicate?
Really? What is it of which I speak?
A scrambling of words describing a
manipulating spider...of sorts.
You know...the *web thing*.

So, it's got the look. And it also has
venom. To play the game...it's way
of life and twisted love. But it's really
not even a type of love. Seduction is
merely an unrehearsed form of false
flattery to oneself. Fear and pain
are the basis of the moves and marks.

A victim attempting to claim a victim.
Now that sounds like an appealing
framework of sound and true relation.
Yes. Once the susceptible might choose
to fall blindly. Proceed through a sure
maze of chaotic, life-consuming events.
Only to end up with a skeleton of an
imagined romance, conjured up by
self-serving desires. And a big fiasco.

Something to be said for being older,
wiser and content with self!
Lordy Mercy!!!

Where Am I Goin'?

He left. He's now with her...
together in heaven. My parents.
I've been so blessed. I could be
confused and overly sad...but I'm not.
They left good instructions. No...
They weren't *into my space*.
But from watching them live...
I've learned the ropes. So...here goes.

Well, in a sense...I'm goin' it alone.
No...no. I don't feel lonely...at least
not right at this moment. I'm sure
there'll be times...and I'll deal with it.
But they were my *immediate family*.
Oh yes. A brother, sister, nieces and
nephews...but miles away. And really
not a part of the threesome we made...
that allowed my survival through a
tough course. And stamina built.

What do we have here? Well...
I have a home. All with respect to
shelter, vicinity and human connections.
With that, I'm very comfortable and happy.
I have talents of which I want to expound.
And there are no binding restraints. God
lead me. A belief system...it's there.
And "Faith, Hope and Love." Yes...

I've got the whole package! How fortunate.
Much gratitude. Now...to always share.
And adhere to responsibilities. Living life.

Funny. Never in my wildest dreams did I
think I could be so stable, secure and certain.
But here I sit with these acquisitions. And at
the same time...I have no idea *where I'm goin'!*
Help me to stay close to you God. I know you'll
never leave me. Thank you.
Hold on...The ride's startin'!!! The future...yep!

Just Feel It

A beginning and an end.
An end and a beginning.
No right or wrong.
Nor good or bad.
Just feel it.

Fear? Not really. More like
slight apprehensive mystery.
To be known? Not yet.
But sure as the past was...
the future will be. And more
than certain. Yet, at this
moment...vague.

Not to run from. No need.
And nowhere to go. Because
here is where it is at. Solid.
But this...this...movement...
breathing whispers with a
tinge of pain. Sorrow?
Perhaps. And rightly so.
Just feel it.

Tomorrow. A new day.
Fresh beginning. But for now...
A night waits to be slept. Safe
and secure...is the fact. Gratitude.
Let the unsteady vibes be siphoned
through the stream of unconsciousness.
To be gone by the morning. And
until slumber falls...
Just feel it.

Time Forward

It's time. Time to move on.
Oh...I'm not relocating. Satisfied
where I live. Stability and sureness
are mine. Must say I've worked
hard for them. In some cases *paid
the price*. And it was worth it.

So now what? Time for action.
I've already thought, dissected,
rehearsed, dealt with, imagined,
prepared and prayed. Do I even
know what I want? Well...hmmm.
Hell yeah! Life to the fullest!

You know what's great? There's
nothing holding me back. No...
Honestly, the only obstacles in my
path are unfounded insecurities.
And those doubts...they are diminishing
day by day. I can say such...and
experience that fact, because my faith
has grown. Faith in my Maker. And
faith in myself.

So, here I go. Or should I say...here I come? Regardless, it's forward motion. Excited? Definitely!
If we meet...I hope I can share with you, the love and care so many people in my past have expressed toward me. And my time forward will be worthy. Blessed to be blessed.

Passion's Friend

Hidden. Lost. Destroyed.
Forgotten. Unaccepted. Unclaimed.
Regardless the reason...untapped the state.
To die with such an excess of untainted
royalties, would seem a wasteful sin.
Would it be? God? Would it be?

The life lived...mostly survival mode.
What now? Lighter days. A softer sense of
being. A love of self...as well as others. A
long time coming...to look in the mirror with
fondness. Hard fought...the acquisition of a
kinder, gentler mind-set.

And now what? To share. To receive.
To be so bold as *chances taken*?
Times before have met with the positive
and the negative. Experiences to grow.
But until now, never totally free from
ever revolving *thought traps*.

Again. What now? Where does passion go
to meet a friend? Oh...the many answers
to a naked question. But really. Really.
Back to God. The gifts are from above.
This trip...this life...I believe there are reasons
for. Answers to why. I have to continue to
live, believing the intense fervor will not
simply be a bittersweet fantasy. Time will tell.
God?

Get Gone!

And it lurks around waiting to pounce.
The good. The future. Fun times ahead.
Things look bright. Been a long time
coming. Uh-oh...apprehension.
Kinda scary. Oh...**that's real good**.

You know. One can be confident and
scared shitless at the same time. Well.
That's profound! Ah...too true.
So...why? Getting back into the social.
Yikes! Like stated...been so long.

Oh...there are the stable and secure
family and friends already in place.
But not necessarily a peer group.
It's the bicycle thing. Yes. Getting
back on the bike...to ride!

So, new people to meet. That's good.
Fear...Get Gone! New and different
places to go. That's good. Fear...
Get Gone! Change of *stuck in the mud*
habits. That's good. Wait a minute.
Change?! Ugh. No. That's good.
Fear...Get Gone! Taking the plunge.

This write...the act of purging fear.
Feel better already. Thanks for listening!
Self, hear self.

My Street...Wooten Road

I grew up in the city. Well, in the city limits.
Really, it was more of a rural setting back
then. We were just inside the west of the
city proper. Our house was set on about a
two and half acre tract of land. That's how the
property was split-up. With a horse pasture next
to our home, it did seem like we were *in
the country*. (Just to note: driveways in
Southeast Texas were covered with oyster
shells...clam shells, if you could afford.)
The ditches lining the road could be fairly
deep. All the crawfish you wanted to catch.
But none to eat.

Actually, to my knowledge our property
was once a fig orchard. There must be
some truth. I know in mowing the yard,
we would scalp the top of the one-time rows.
At least that was early on. Finally, after
years of being mown, the rows leveled out.
Basically, Talah trees...(not sure of that spelling).
Anyway, we called them Chinaberry. And some
pines. But mostly just a lot of tall grass and weeds.
Bonus...in the spring, lots of Dewberries.
Dodging the ant beds.

We lived south of Highway 90. Not too
far past the intersection of the highway
and Major Dr. The last route of the
school bus...in that direction. Our house
was about half a mile down the road...
Wooten Rd. At the end, after crossing
Washington Blvd. (a prestigious name
for the narrow road), through the
brushes was a rice canal...where daring
kids would *shoot the flumes*.

In my younger years, there were probably
about 18 houses scattered along the half
mile stretch. Each property had plenty
of yard for us kids to play, without
fear of...well, basically very little traffic.
To tell others how to get to our house...
we said "Just turn at Weidel's Washeteria."
Important: Weidel's had the closest Coke
machine. But walking down the rough,
hot asphalt road meant few trips for the
coveted drink.

The next street over was Reynolds.
Its definite claim to fame...in the
early 70's, the Catholic Church built
a KC Hall. And it had a swimming pool!!!
Being the Southern Baptist we were, we
didn't have a membership. But on
occasion friends would invite. Mostly
I just sweated out the hot, humid summers
and dreamt of jumping off the diving board.

My Dad always planted a garden. Really, it wasn't one of those big, sprawling gardens. But just enough for us to have plenty of tomatoes, peppers, cucumbers and cantaloupe. So hard to make something of the cement gumbo, unless a lot of toil and effort was put to the cause. Instead, he built...by his own design and unique imagination...a plastic-covered, wire greenhouse. It did us kids a lot of good... growing and selling tomato and bell pepper plants to Jefferson Feed and Gibson's nursery. The main purpose was to give my Grandpa Bowling a hobby when he lived the winters with us. And we did profit to each of our small change purses.

Our particular neighborhood...at least the several houses surrounding...was *tight*. We had get-togethers especially during the summer and holidays. Food, food, food. My Dad's specialty... barbeque chicken. And for my Mother...it was her homemade peach ice cream! Funny, all the women on Wooten Road could cook!! And sometimes we gathered for birthday parties. No, not the kind with beer kegs. Remember, most of us Southern Baptist. But one neighbor man kept a steady supply of Texas Pride!

One of the highlights of a spring or summer weekend, was the possibility of watching skydivers float to the ground. We called them parachuters...for what that's worth. The Beaumont Municipal Airport was a bit further west of Wooten... on the north side of Hwy 90. Now, I say *float to the ground*...but we couldn't see them past the tree line. The color chutes were spectacular to a child. Another summer happening...Gateway Fireworks. If we didn't get to go, we could see a few of the *high ones*. And one of the neighbor boys always managed to finagle his parents to let him sit atop their roof to watch. If lucky, I got to join in.

Well, these are some memories of *my street* on which I lived growing up. Friends from the past, who will be friends forever. Good times and bad times. But the best memory...a safe, long road to ride my blue Schwinn bicycle. *And I have to mention...* that soft, green San Augustine grass and clover. Barefoot...naturally! (oh yeah...bee stings!!)

The Flame of Shame

Four burners on a gas stove.
In the past, all turned up to the
highest degree. Burning within
and without. Burning holes.
Burning the soul. And burning
down...almost everything. But not.

Years pass, and all the while cooking
continues. Life continues. The cook
is sometimes likened to a chef. But
not. Just an everyday, life-sustaining,
incredibly good cook. Knowing when to
turn the heat on and when to turn it off.

So, the stove...it sits there. It has its
place in the house. What has become a
kind, delightful and safe home. Three
of the burners can be turned all the way
off. But one...just one remains lit. Even
if it's barely seen or felt. And most
days...it's neither. But its life...is part of
life. It just is.

Today, while the tiny blue color lightly
burned as always... Today, some grease
splattered and the flame more than flickered.
It jumped up and scorched. The child yelled.
The pain felt...used to be the norm. But not

anymore. Thank God. Yet, this afternoon
the flame of shame produced such discomfort.
It has been a long while since exposure to
the useless, destructive, pitiful feel.

With the color of orange returning to blue...
rest and recuperate. It will happen again.
Oh, every once in awhile...no matter how
good the culinary skills...there'll at least be
a singe. I'd rather have a working stove to
cook and eat...with possibilities of flare-ups.
Than an empty gas tank and a hungry stomach.
And what about warmth? Yes, I want to be warm.

This cook doesn't know how to turn all the
burners off completely. Thus avoiding accidents.
And I'm glad. What's that called? Being alive.
Living life. A life worth living. Grateful.

When You Get To Say "Thank You"

Be gracious? Of course. It's what most of us were taught from childhood. Sometimes it's easy...and sometimes it's hard. The words need to come from the heart. Although, many times they are just a repetitious and narrow courtesy. Make us feel good, complete and sometimes...*off the hook*.

So, someone has done something for us. Yes. It can be that another's actions have blessed us immensely. Going further... perhaps saved our life. At any rate, we are for the better because of their efforts, generosity and care. How fortunate we are. A person has given of themselves for our benefit. Yes. Thanks indeed.

Sometimes...at that time...when we receive... we don't have the words. You know... we don't understand the depth of the gift. Or we have trouble articulating. Maybe we tell of our appreciation...but it seems so lacking. There are instances when all we can do is say *thank you*...when our being says...*THANK YOU...you are SO important to me at this time!* But we can only say *thank you*...and know that we mean it with all our heart.

Years pass. Growth occurs. Stability ensues.
Hooray!!!!!! The hard has gotten easier.
People have helped us learn how to help
ourselves. The *neediness* of another's *ok*
is no longer necessary. We like ourselves.
We like others. We are equal to humanity.
Flaws in those we think highly of, do not
disturb us. Their faults don't frighten our
belief in self...nor our belief in them. It's
called living life.

We can now say THANK YOU. And
we know the person on the receiving end...
Well...they know we've made it. We survived.
We overcame obstacles. We beat our demons.
Indeed...So Grateful! Yes, there'll be rocky
times in the future. But we'll once again use
what they've taught us. So many people in
my life that I want to be able to thank. Mostly
impossible. I just pray that somehow they know
they made a difference in the positive.

But on this day...I get to *thank* one who can
hear. I feel so privileged to do so. In fact,
there is an aura of feel-good all around me.
So to one of my guides along my journey...
Thank You Carol! Blessings to you!

This Quiet Winter

It's after deaths...and before a new life.
Ducks are in a row. The future...hmmm.
Right now just biding time. Apprehension
and lack of certainty surfaces occasionally.
Just surfaces...not to overwhelm. Priceless.
Yes. To not know and remain even keel. Nice.

Night happens a lot. Because sleep happens
during much of the day. Maybe a downfall of
sorts. But not a depressive scene. More mild
lethargy. Well...sorta. Oh, I don't know. Who
knows? Think outside the mental health box.
Right!!!! It's just where I'm at. My recent life:
losses, changes, learning to adapt, taking chances.
Just a couple of years ago, anxiety would sweep.
But not. No. Not now. Grateful.

Cold, snowy days and nights. Much of the time
indoors and alone. But not lonely. Yes...a
quiet winter. Waiting for spring...but not
ready for it. When spring *springs*...game on.
But for now...silence. Looking forward to share.
Share life, heart, passion. Someone special?
Perhaps. If meant to be. Regardless, I consider
myself pretty special. Ah… That's the secret!

Boredom doesn't seem to lurk. But a bit more activity...a probable notion to action. At any rate, this quiet winter...I have Peace. Once this mind screamed for a steadiness. Never imagined more. And now...Now Peace...encompassing This Quiet Winter. God Is Good.

Cultivating Identity

Some people know who they are,
what they want, how to express their
being...in the labor delivery room.
Well...you get the gist.

Then there are others who gradually
grow...in an *appropriate* timely
manner. Soon learn rights, wrongs,
cues, clues...all leading to making
their place in life. Stabilization clicks.

What about the late bloomers? You
know...the very late bloomers. The
ones who change their college major
several times...perhaps never to graduate.
But they get the *education* that affords
them a purposeful and meaningful
life. Bumps and bruises soon to heal.
All in all...on a fairly consistent track
by age 35 - 40.

AND THEN. God help! (Hint: He has
helped!) Then there are those whose heart
beats by the seat of their pants. Nothing's
for sure. Always starting over...after the fall.
There is no clarity in who they are, what their
purpose is or where they're going. Prone to
unwise choices and accepting bread crumbs.

Shit! Damn! This sounds bad. Not very promising...and such a waste! Ahh...but hold on. There's something to this kind of life. See...because of how the cards have been dealt...you come to realize you get a new deck every day! Yeah. When you have to continue to start over out of absolute necessity...you learn that you can also start over when you just want things to get even better! Well...that's grand!

So, here at age 57...A life that I desire is beginning. I do not look at the past as a disaster...rather a continuous, extremely rough cultivation period. Every pain, mistake made, feeling hurt, burned bridge and brief loss of sanity...well, it didn't break me! I survived. Not only survival...but my formation. And a sound and solid foundation...earned. Slowly, I'm realizing how I want to present myself to the world. As a complete person. **Hell...Maslow's got nothin' on me!!!!!**

I Never Knew...And Now I Do

All my life...I never knew. Words, definitions, meanings...a whole dictionary full. Plus all the slang! Thing is, I never really understood the definition of neurosis. Hmmm. Now, I can hear you...And?

Well, somehow I just always thought neurosis was a fear of reality. Perhaps it is. Oh, I don't know. I just know that about a year ago, I got more than curious... and looked up the definition. Surprise!!! It is much more about perceiving things in a negative fashion. So, I let this sink in a bit. **Ta-da!!!!** Light Bulbs!!!!!

At that point I started realizing that every thought, notion, even any stimuli that I felt or experienced had a good chance of triggering a negative thought or mood. In most cases, a minute thought or visualization would occur...and immediately there would be a *dip* towards the negative in my present emotion.

THIS had been going on since October 28, 1961. No lie! (Get it...my birthday) With this insight, I realized that I could possibly manipulate my thinking...catch it when it happened...and diffuse the heavy, cumbersome *albatross*. So, I started.

First occurrence...I was sitting playing solitaire at the truck stop...on the iPad. In split seconds, a thought followed by a *dip* happened. Now, let me back up...this happened continuously. But now I was seeing it for what it was. Anyhoo... I believe the thought was something similar to... I need to wash my hair. I need to wash my hair *went to* I have to wash my hair. That *went to* I don't want to wash my hair. (I'll cut through this shit.) It ended up...I'm a loser if I don't wash my hair. I'm gonna end up in a deep depression if I don't wash my hair. GOD HELP!!!!!! Yucky feeling in the pit of my stomach.

Well, well. What have we here? Oh, just the typical nut job. You gotta laugh to not cry! Really people! You do! So, anyway...I wouldn't be beat. At that moment I was able to tell myself... Having dirty hair...or not wanting to wash my hair...that has nothing to do with this bad feeling. There is no reason to feel bad. There is no basis for this bad feeling. So...Away with it!!!! People...let me explain...the neurotic feeling was not just negative in simple terms. It was a feeling of doom borderline despair. AND I'd done this to myself all my life. Whew!

Anyway, given this example...I told myself that not washing my hair did not certify me to feel despair. I started visualizing this and saying this. And by God...**it worked!!!** I disconnected the relay that went from thought to emotion. The relay was false and defective. As the days went on, I didn't push it. I just let myself process in my mind, when the situation occurred. And folks it wasn't about washing my hair...it was connected to anything and everything. I had always lived in a steady state of negative.

Sure. I could be positive and upbeat. I could carry on and make light. Life happened and I just went through the motions. Good times and bad times. But I never realized how I was constantly set up to *dip*. It was all so vague. But not anymore. In fact, at this point... it has all but been extinguished. HOORAY!!!!!

So, my onion. What??? Oh. So, my life.
The constant peeling of the onion. Yep. When I was 20 years old I started getting psychiatric help. I started out with clinical depression and it has flourished tremendously into 3+ significant disorders. I'm joking people! Well, I'm not. But I'm laughing because today I can laugh! And add the ever-present neurosis...which to my understanding is not a diagnosable disorder as such. It's just a little icing on the cake. Just to make life more bizarre!

**Bottom line: I don't have to feel bad, when there is no reason to feel bad...ANYMORE!!! YAY!!!!
And yes...isn't God Good?!!**
(This writing is repetitive of an earlier writing.
I'm Glad! Lets me know the change stuck.)

The Evolving Door

So much has been thought.
So much has been felt.
Actions taken. Positive and
negative consequences.
Having been acted upon...
again, good and bad results.
And this is the way it should
be...to live a life.

Six years ago, the pen became
a friend. To write. To expel.
To expose. Searching, hiding,
hanging on. Crying in despair.
The exorcism of an identity
which harbored fear, assumed
inaccurately...always to the
detriment.

Now, going on three years...
it has been a matter of *brushing up*.
Eliminating the scattered debris from
disorders which were finally put
in order. Or more wonderfully...
overcome! A maintenance plan
for the future...a must. Indeed in
place. So grateful. And thankful
for others.

Nice to not be making the same
mistakes. Making mistakes...yes.
But not *the same ole*...
And being easy on self. Instead of
an internal cruel master of hopelessness.

Yes, it has been an evolution. Days
continue to get better. No. Not always
the best of days. But clearly a stable,
sane handle on life. To share is in order.
Let another know...all is not lost. No
matter how dark...there can be light.

So with all being written...
And all being said...
Wake up each day and live what
has been learned. Affording one
to lay down at night in peace.
Always to give God the glory and
the praise.

So...I get the *evolving*...but the *door*?
Oh yes...this door opens to a bright
future. **It's just a beginning!**

www.ingramcontent.com/pod-product-compliance
Lightning Source LLC
Chambersburg PA
CBHW032337300426
44109CB00041B/1090